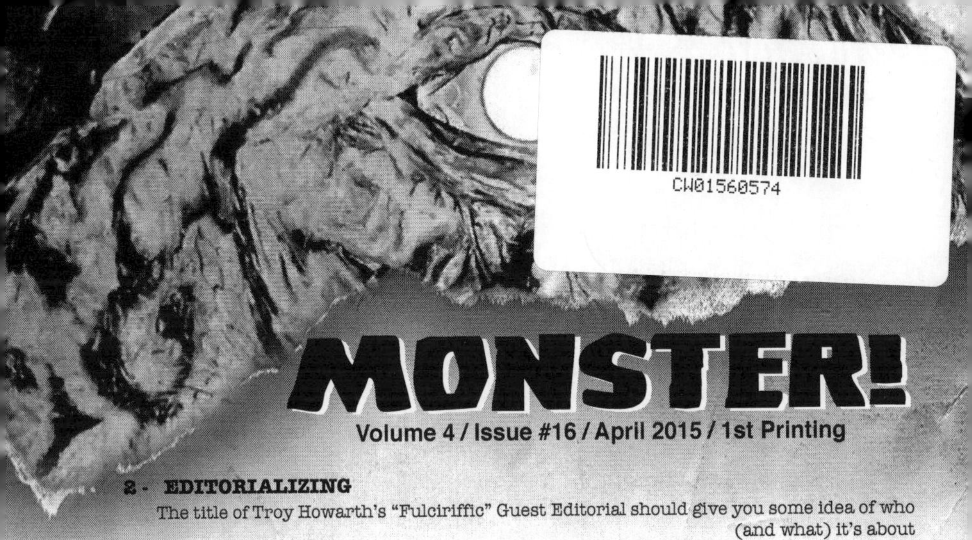

MONSTER!

Volume 4 / Issue #16 / April 2015 / 1st Printing

Artwork: Michael Elvidge (p.5)

Contributors: Mark Savage, Dawn Dabell, José Cruz, Bill Adcock, Stephen R. Bissette, Eric Messina, Adam Parker-Edmondston, Troy Howarth, Dennis Capicik, Christos Mouroukis, Les Moore, Brian Harris, Steve Fenton, and Tim Paxton

Timothy Paxton, Editor & Design Demon / Steve Fenton, Editor & Info-wrangler
Tony Strauss, Edit-fiend • Brian Harris, El Publisher de Grand Poobah

MONSTER! is published monthly. Subscriptions are NOT available.

Editorializing

A FULCIRIFFIC GUEST EDITORIAL

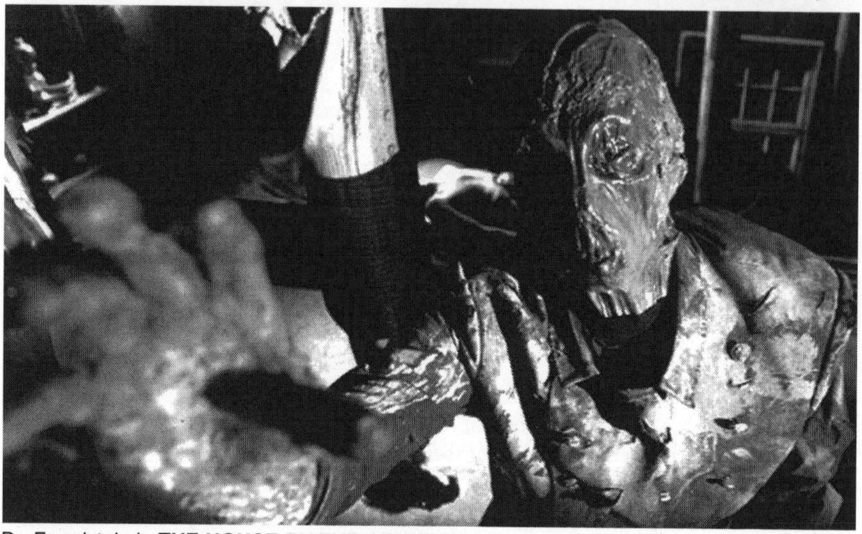

Dr. Freudstein in **THE HOUSE BY THE CEMETERY**. The same actor, Giovanni de Nava, also played the zombified Schweick in Fulci's **THE BEYOND**

Welcome to the latest issue of *Monster!* My name is Troy Howarth, and I will be your tour guide. I propose to spend the next few paragraphs talking about Lucio Fulci. Why Fulci, you ask? *Why the hell not!* Of all the key figures associated with the Italian horror film, I would argue that Fulci is the one who is the most associated with monsters—zombies, specifically. Mario Bava and Riccardo Freda kicked the trend off in the late 1950s, but Freda was resolutely uninterested in the supernatural and Bava only sporadically incorporated monsters into his work: Man was monstrous enough for him. Antonio Margheriti specialized in space operas more than horror and, of course, Dario Argento has typically worked in the more "realistic" (*ha!*) confines of the *giallo*. By contrast, Lucio Fulci lighted upon the zombie subgenre late in his career, and the living dead would cast a long shadow over the remainder of his prolific and pleasingly eclectic filmography.

Truth be told, my decision to focus on Fulci is also purely selfish. As some of you may be aware, I have already written books on Bava (*The Haunted World of Mario Bava*), the *giallo* (*So Deadly, So Perverse*) and the horror genre in general (*The Tome of Terror: Horror Films of the 1930s*, co-written with my good friend, Chris Workman). My next project, as it happens, is *Splintered Visions: Lucio Fulci and His Films*. I came to the project somewhat by chance: following the completion of *So Deadly*, my publisher talked to me about potential follow-up subjects and let it be known that he really, really wanted to do a book on Dario Argento. I love Argento—at least, his work through the 1990s—but I felt that the topic had been done to death; why not Fulci, I replied? It didn't take a whole lot of convincing before I got the greenlight to proceed. I then set out to do the most comprehensive and in-depth analysis of Fulci's career as a writer and director that has ever been written in English. That doesn't sound very modest, I'll grant you, but it's true. I had long admired Stephen Thrower's *Beyond Terror*, but felt it—like most everything else ever written about Fulci in English—was a little too focused on the director's horror movies. The truth of the matter is, Fulci had been in the business for 30 years by the time he found cult horror movie stardom with the release of **ZOMBIE** (a.k.a. *Zombi 2*, 1979, Italy [see *M!* #13, p.59]), and a good chunk of his earlier career had been spent in writing and directing comedies. Fulci was a jack-of-all-trades: he made westerns, musicals, sci-fi, action films, etc. There's little denying that he had a particular flair for the dark and the violent, but viewers only familiar with his gory horror movies may well be surprised by the lightness of touch he displayed in so many of his earlier works. What started off as a fairly straightforward "films of" book soon mutated into something more when I hooked up with

Mike Baronas, whose passion for all things Fulci is possibly even greater than my own. Mike's extensive contacts in the film convention scene allowed me access to a ton of actors and technicians who worked with Fulci, so I found myself interviewing everybody from Richard Johnson and Catriona MacColl to Franco Nero and Paolo Malco. It was a new and exhilarating experience for me, and I could not be more pleased with the end result. No book should ever purport to be "definitive", but I sincerely feel that *Splintered Visions* deserves a spot on the book shelves of everybody who calls themselves a Fulci fan.

Still, it would be highly inappropriate to spend the entire editorial pimping my book or dwelling on films that fall outside the scope of the *Monster!* mission statement. If you're holding this magazine and reading these words, there's a very good chance that you are more than familiar with such Fulci horrors as **ZOMBIE**, **CITY OF THE LIVING DEAD** (*Paura nella città dei morti viventi*, 1980, Italy), **THE BEYOND** (*...E tu vivrai nel terrore! L'aldilà*, 1981, Italy) and **THE HOUSE BY THE CEMETERY** (*Quella villa accanto al cimitero*, 1981, Italy). Critical reaction to these films is typically mixed, and for understandable reasons. They are mood pieces with an emphasis on images of death and decay. They are renowned for their shocking highlights and belittled for their admittedly minimalist narratives. They are also loaded with some of the coolest "monster" makeup and gore effects you're ever likely to see. Suffice it to say, there's a good reason why these films are still talked about in revered tones in one corner, while openly derided and ridiculed in other circles.

The zombie is an obvious metaphor for the fear of death and the great beyond. As human beings, we have established an elaborate framework of beliefs and principles which protect us from these fears; it can be argued that religion itself is designed to shield us from the horrific possibility that life on earth as we know it may well be it—no celestial choirs, no drifting through time and space and getting closer to a benevolent creator. Still, I have no desire to get too philosophical or controversial: whatever one may or may not choose to believe, most of us have a definite fear of death and dying. Myths like the zombie or the vampire allow us to explore the potential of life after death, though paradoxically these scenarios posit on the notion of destroying the lives of others in order to sustain our own. The zombie myth extends well beyond motion pictures, but first started to really penetrate the public consciousness thanks to the release of Victor Halperin's independent horror hit **WHITE ZOMBIE** (1932, USA), with Bela Lugosi as a dastardly villain who uses voodoo to enslave his enemies. Other zombie films would emerge in the '40s and '50s, ranging from the sublime (**I WALKED WITH A ZOMBIE**, 1943, D: Jacques Tourneur) to the ridiculous (**VOODOO ISLAND**, 1957, D: Reginald LeBorg), but it was the release of George A. Romero's **NIGHT OF THE LIVING DEAD** (1968, USA) that really turned the tide. Romero and company made this watershed horror classic on the cheap in rural Pennsylvania and were not even able to enjoy its surprise commercial success owing to a SNAFU with the copyright notice, but the film's impact on the horror genre proved to be immense. The Italians, never keen to avoid exploiting a popular cinematic movement, eventually hopped on the bandwagon with Jorge Grau's magnificent **LET SLEEPING CORPSES LIE** (*Non si deve profanare il sonno dei morti*, a.k.a. **THE LIVING DEAD AT THE MANCHESTER MORGUE**, 1974, Italy/Spain), but it took the release of Romero's eye-popping **NOTLD** follow-up, **DAWN OF THE DEAD** (*Zombi*, 1978, Italy/USA), to really open the floodgates. Released in Italy as **ZOMBI**, Romero's film mixed pointed sociopolitical satire with gut-munching special effects and proved to be a box office smash. It didn't take long for the Italians to respond with **ZOMBI 2**... or **ZOMBIE**, as it would become known in the

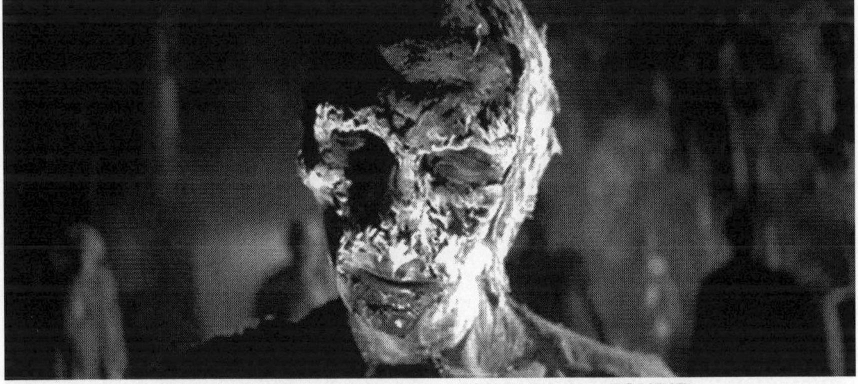

The dead walk in Fulci's classic **ZOMBI 2** (a.k.a. **ZOMBIE**)

United States. Romero and his Italian co-producer Dario Argento (then enjoying his tenure as Italy's reigning *Maestro* of Horror) were none too pleased by the cheekiness of the title and tried to press charges, but it was decided that the word "*zombi*" was public property, and the film would go on to become a major box office triumph in its own right. The film allowed Fulci to claim his perch as Argento's main competitor, and the middle-aged filmmaker suddenly found himself being fêted in genre magazines like *Fangoria*. The truth of the matter is, Fulci was not even the original choice to direct **ZOMBIE**: Enzo G. Castellari (best known for his stylish actioners like **STREET LAW** [*Il cittadino si ribella*, 1974, Italy]) passed on directing the film and suggested Fulci, who was then going through a bit of a slump thanks to the failure of his ambitious and rather costly *giallo*, **THE PSYCHIC** (*Sette notte in nero*, 1977, Italy). It proved to be a match made in heaven: Fulci took to the genre like a (tortured) duck to water…and the rest, as they say, is history.

Sadly, many critics would lazily parrot the same claims against Fulci over and over again: that he was a hack who lacked in originality, that he was a rip-off artist, etc. Truth be told, a brief comparison of Fulci's zombie films with those of Romero reveals very little in the way of "sampling". As Fulci was always quick to point out, Romero did not invent the zombie mythos, though he did introduce the idea of the zombie-as-cannibal. Fulci would cram plenty of flesh-eating into his zombie movies, but the similarities more or less end on that level. Romero's films are cheerfully satirical, whereas Fulci's are steeped in images of death and decay. Romero's movies are built on montage, while Fulci's are moodier and more atmospheric. It's quite possible to love them both—lord knows, I do—but there's little doubt that they each had their own specific strengths and weaknesses as filmmakers and dramatists. For Romero, the zombies would become a metaphor for man's inability to communicate with his fellow man; for Fulci, they represented a grim foreshadowing of what we we're all destined to become.

Inevitably, the argument will continue long after this editorial is forgotten: Romero vs. Fulci, who was better? At one point I would have argued for Romero, but the process of writing *Splintered Visions* has convinced me that Fulci was The Man. He had such a tremendous versatility and was equally at home in other genres compared to his beloved living dead pictures. Indeed, I actually prefer his work in the *giallo* and the Spaghetti Western subgenres, to say nothing of such standalone titles as his historical drama **BEATRICE CENCI** (1969, Italy) and his political sex comedy **THE EROTICIST** (*All'onorevole piacciono le donne [Nonostante le apparenze... e purche la nazione non lo sappia]*, 1972, Italy). Still, I would hate to stoop to bad-mouthing Romero in order to make Fulci shine more brightly. They are both on my list of ten favorite directors, they both made their mark and continue to be influential and they both made films I hold near and dear. Still, the tedious argument that Fulci was a derivative hack needs to die a speedy death. There is virtually nothing of Romero or Argento to be seen in Fulci's horror films and *gialli*; some elements were unavoidable since they were setting the trends that Fulci was obliged to follow, but beyond that they couldn't have been more dissimilar. Argento was cool and precise, whereas Fulci was hot-blooded and prone to hyperbole. Romero could get down-and-dirty, as evidenced by **DAY OF THE DEAD** (1985, USA), but most of his work has a gentler, EC-Comics vibe; he speaks broadly and uses caricature for comic effect. Fulci had a flair for comedy, but his horror movies tend to be deadly serious—even if their excesses sometimes bordered on the absurd. Horror fans just love to pit icons against each other, but I've never understood the need for it myself. Hammer versus Universal? Karloff versus Lugosi? Screw that...I love 'em *all*!

Fulci often described himself as a Catholic who wished he did not believe in God. As he got older and his health started to decline, his relationship with death would become closer, more intimate. His later, reviled works may be rough around the edges, but, if seen in the right light, they have some unexpectedly moving flourishes. Movies like **AENIGMA** (1987, Italy/Yugoslavia), **THE HOUSE OF CLOCKS** (*La casa nel tempo*, 1989, Italy) and **VOICES FROM BEYOND** (*Voci dal profondo*, 1991, Italy) may lack the sheen and polish of his peak period works, but they have an elegiac quality that can only be explained by the fact that Fulci realized he was, in essence, staring death in the face. The concept of being trapped in a failing body was something he was living with on a daily basis: his mind remained sharp and his wit as acerbic as ever, but diabetes and hepatitis slowly destroyed him on a physical level and depression began to creep in. These later films deal even more explicitly with the concept of the temporal nature of our existence and extend a kind of optimism that there may be something beyond the veils of this world and that it may even be possible to retain some level of contact with our loved ones on earth. Was it a sincere conviction, or merely whistling past the graveyard? Only Fulci could have answered that question for sure. The films themselves, however, are richer and more rewarding than many critics would have us believe.

The same can be said for Fulci's filmography as a whole, however. As time has gone on, Fulci's cult "value" has continued to soar, whereas time and a number of wretched movies have taken some of the luster away from Argento. It is not likely that Fulci will ever be given the full measure of respect he truly deserves from snobby mainstream critics, but in a sense that is neither here nor there: so long as fans continue to carry the torch... *Fulci Lives!*

WANTED! More Readers Like Sinistre Droolette from Corps-Nue-dans-un-Champ, France, who sez, "Ooh-la-la, my favorite film mags are *Monster!* and *Weng's Chop*"

WANTED! More readers like Noze Feratoo of Walla Walla, Washington

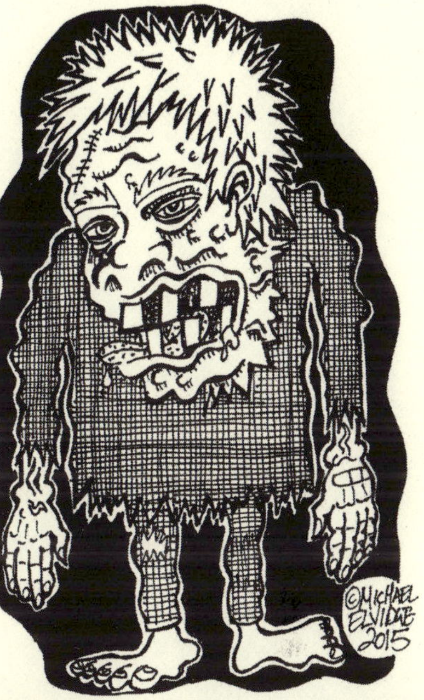

WANTED! More Readers Like Mongo McGillicutty

WANTED! More Readers Like Andrew Cook

(*"Adventure at the Centre of the Earth"*)

Reviewed by Steve Fenton

Mexico, 1964. D: Alfredo B. Crevenna

AACDLT's batty brute totes swooning Kitty de Hoyos back to the bat-cave in this monstrously marvelous still scanned from an ancient issue of *Famous Monsters*

Okay, purely in the interests of some self-indulgent personal nostalgia, there now follows a greatly elaborated- and expanded-upon revision of a review I originally hacked out for the very first ish of my long-gone-and-largely-unlamented Mexi-movie 'zine, *¡Panicos!* Never mind done on a word processor (or even a typewriter, for that matter), issue #1 of said zine (dating from 1989) was, primitively enough...*hand*-written, no less! It was an idea I "borrowed"—simply because I didn't have any other option at the time—from the minimalist, manually scrawled NYC-based sleazoid cinema mini-'zine known as *Grindhouse* ("co-edited" [if that's the correct term!] by one "Rat" and J. Adler, it gained some notoriety within the cult movie 'zine scene at that time as one of the smuttiest/sleaziest 'zines around, and it didn't even have any pictures in it, just psychotically-scrawled text of a decidedly non-PC nature. It should not be confused with another, far-less-scuzzy 'zine from the same period out of Ellenville, New York called *The Grindhouse Journal*, self-published by a certain Fidge Dextro). What were my reasons for hand-lettering *¡Panicos!* #1? I think maybe my Smith Corona electric must have clapped out on me—possibly it may have just run out of ribbon (i.e., ink)?—or I was unable to afford a PC yet or something; but all that's neither here nor there now. It's time to take a trip, not back to the early days/ dark ages of my still-ongoing 'zining obsession, but to the very center of the Earth itself! Ready or not...here we go!

Lorena Velázquez as space babe Beta and the bulbous-brained alien Tagual, from **LA NAVE DE LOS MONSTRUOS** (1960). The same creature also later turned up in **SANTO AND BLUE DEMON VS. THE MONSTERS** (*Santo y Blue Demon contra los monstrous*, 1970). Both films are true way-out, wacky wonders of Mexi-monster madness!

An introductory word-crawl which includes *mucho* ominous narration *en Español* (e.g., "*...ataques de los feroces y monstruosos animales...*" [Hmmm, wonder what that means?]) kicks off this way-out, wacky, wild and wonderful chunk of primo South-of-the-Border monster schlock. As a matter of fact, along with Rogelio A. González's **LA NAVE DE LOS MONSTRUOS** (*"The Ship of Monsters"*), that film's same director González's **EL CONQUISTADOR DE LA LUNA** (*"Conqueror of the Moon"* [both 1960]) and Julián Soler's **LOCURA DE TERROR** (*"Terror Madness"* [1961]), our present flick ranks right up at the top of my long list of Mexploitation monster faves (in this case those not also involving masked wrestlers, which are generally the kind that ought to be tops on anybody's list, if they've got any bad taste whatsoever).

By no means coincidentally, our present title and all three others mentioned in the preceding paragraph were produced by Jesús Sotomayor Martínez and written or co-written in collaboration with another writer by José María Fernández Unsáin (1918-1997). All those except for **AVENTURA AL CENTRO DE LA TIERRA** were jointly penned by Fernández Unsáin and his frequent writing collaborator Alfredo Varela (1912-1986).

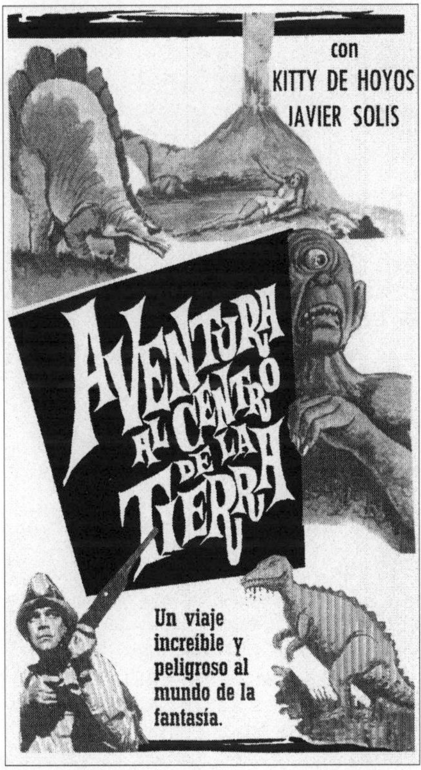

A crowd of tourists, not heeding the dramatic opening narrator and Raúl Lavista's accompanying "eerie" theme music—as if they weren't fair warning enough—is conducted on a guided tour of Cacahuamilpa Caverns ("*¡Fantastico!*"). Situated in Guerrero, Mexico amidst the Sierra Madre del Sur, Grutas de Cacahuamilpa National Park is best-known for the caverns for which it earned its name. One of the biggest and most elaborate cave systems on the planet, the Grutas de Cacahuamilpa system comes complete with a pair of underground rivers that over the eons have eroded tunnels through the very living rock itself, and it is a popular tourist attraction where visitors may camp-out on the

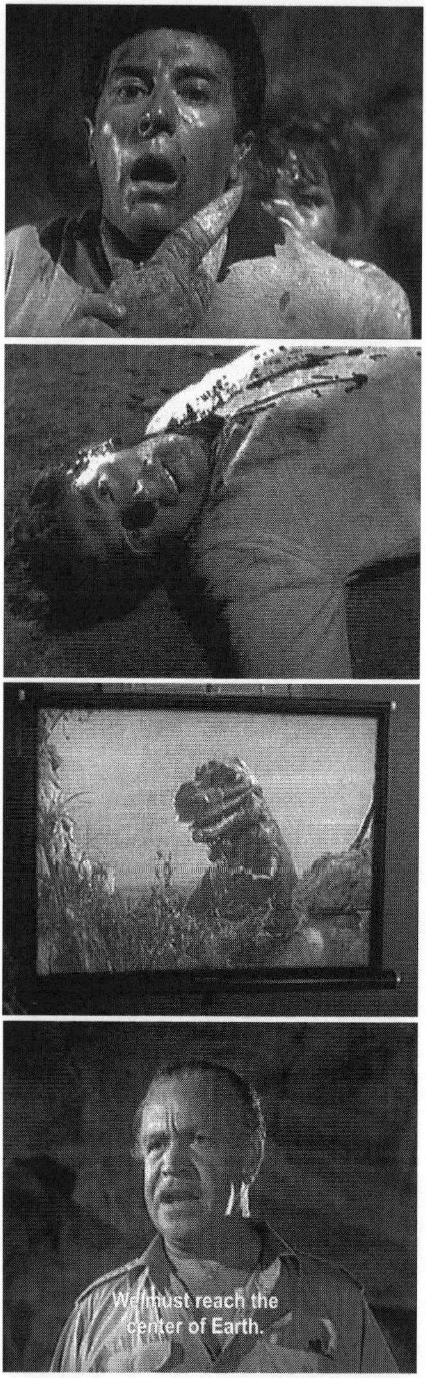
We must reach the
center of Earth.

Various screen shots from **AACDLT**. The top shot shows Carlos Nieto and Carmen Molina, in jeopardy; the bottom one depicts José Elías Moreno as the *intrepido* Prof. Díaz

grounds to go rock climbing, rappelling and spelunking, or simply explore the area's many natural wonders, such as its exotic geological formations. According to Wikipedia, "This section of the Sierra Madre del Sur is made of rock, mostly limestone, that was formed under oceans millions of years ago. The caverns extend through the municipalities of Pilcaya, Tetipac and Taxco of Guerrero state, and extend into Morelos state in the municipality of Coatlán del Río. The parks extends over 2,700 hectares of land, and is located southwest of Mexico City, near the silversmithing town of Taxco". Hence, what better setting than such terrain for a cinematic scenario about explorers who discover a lost world detached from both civilization and even time itself?

Bored by the Cacahuamilpa tour-guide's monotonous rambling, a pair of starry-eyed young lovers sneak off to a secluded "shady nook" among the stalagmites for a discreet necking session. "This is not the right place for kissing", she says, making coy. "I love to kiss you *anywhere*", he replies, his passions aroused. Just when we're wondering exactly where he might be about to kiss her next, from the extreme foreground at bottom-left of the frame, a latex-looking bestial claw reaches in, unseen by the understandably preoccupied neckers. Oblivious to this shadow-obscured whatsit which is lurking well within arm's reach of them, the girl, Julia (Carmen Molina, who does a commendably convincing job of acting terrified when the time comes; and you can be sure it does), coquettishly frolics off still deeper into the cave, only to stumble into a deep, dark hole; down which her boyfriend (Carlos Nieto) soon follows her (there may indeed be some sort of dark Freudian psychological symbology afoot here, but I guess I shouldn't read too much into things, although sometimes it's great fun to do so, even if it is mostly all just in our one-track minds). After the traditional "slap-the-hysterical-female-to-snap-her-back-to-her-senses" scene, the lovers are promptly set upon by a just-out-of-frame, scream-inducing and clearly very non-human assailant. That same rubbery talon glimpsed a short time earlier causes some spraying jugular gore which somehow looks all the more gruesome for being depicted in glorious B&W (as is the rest of the film. For my *dinero*, most of the greatest Mexploitation *peliculas*—especially those of the horror/monster kind—come in monochrome).

From the murder scene, a plaster cast of one of the monster's footprints is made and hurried to the inevitable wise old academician, one Professor Díaz (René Cardona, Sr.'s **SANTA CLAUS** [1959] himself, José Elías Moreno [1910-1969] yet again; his appearances in *mucho* maxi-Mexploitation are

Ramón Bugarini bites the big one—or rather, *it* bites him—in one of the numerous thrilling moments to be found in **AVENTURA AL CENTRO DE LA TIERRA**

legion. In addition to playing Father Christmas, he later went on to play the mad *medico* who creates the monstrous apeman "Gomar the Gorilla" [Gerardo Zepeda] in Cardona, Sr.'s **NIGHT OF THE BLOODY APES** [*La horripilante bestia humana*, 1969]). In the present film, those wounds on the dead man's throat bespeak of some heretofore unknown species ("No doubt: claw wound" – "A huge claw; a brutal one. Note the jugular, Professor" – "Severed, as with a giant razor" – "What kind of beast did it?" – "I have no idea"). From her hospital bed, mentally shattered survivor Julia gibbers hysterically, rendered mad by the shock of her ordeal in the cavern, where she had witnessed her beau being slaughtered right before her eyes by an unknown whatchamacallit. After her presiding physician prescribes a dose of Sodium Pentothal in hopes of clearing her memory as to what went down way down in the depths of the caves, she still rants incoherently, unable to provide answers. Thus, determined to get to the bottom of the mystery, *el profesor* whips together the typical generic "expedition", then shows its members still *more* stolen footage: yep, there's that 'gator and Gila tussle from Hal Roach's **ONE MILLION B.C.** (1940, USA) once again, for the umpteenth gazillionth time, as well as clips from Jack Bernhard's peachy keen PRC "lost world" fossil **UNKNOWN ISLAND** (1948, USA). Obviously convinced by all the cheap dinosaur FX on display in these stock shots, our human heroes—numbering the aforementioned Prof. Díaz, as well as Dr. Manuel Ríos (Javier Solis), Dr. Peña (Carlos Cortés), Hilda Ramírez and geologist Prof. Laura Ponce (Columba Domínguez), along with speleologist and big game hunter Jaime Rocha (passable "Tricky Dickie" Nixon lookalike David Reynoso)—undertake a subterranean safari down into the caverns, intent on discovering the source of the footprints. "I welcome you on our journey to the center of the Earth", says Elías Moreno as Díaz, addressing we the audience as well as his onscreen colleagues.

Playing the mandatory "intellectual airhead" heroine, Prof. Díaz's personal assistant *señorita* Hilda Ramírez, played by the purrrfect Kitty de Hoyos (Rafael Baledón's **LA LOBA** / "The She-Wolf" [1965] herself!), unwisely goes for a stroll all by her lonesome to snap some photos and in the process gets menaced by a pit of presumably poisonous snakes after slipping and dangling by her hands from a craggy overhang, whereupon she must be rescued by the heroic menfolk. After subsequently developing the film in her camera at their underground bivouac, Hilda discovers she has unknowingly captured an exposure of a pair of strange, inhuman—yet at the same time strangely *human*—eyes peering out of the darkness. Shortly thereafter, more monsterish footprints are found—which it doesn't take a cryptozoologist to realize weren't made by any known species—and this eerie discovery greatly increases the ominous tone

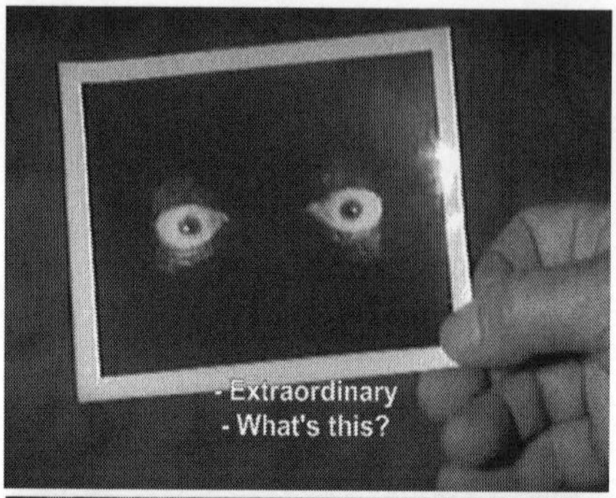

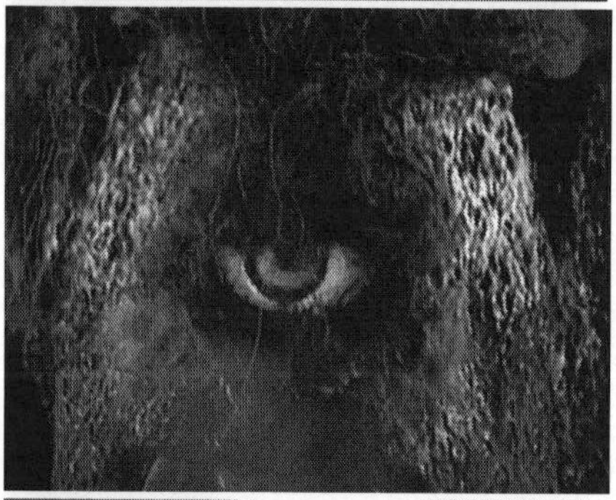

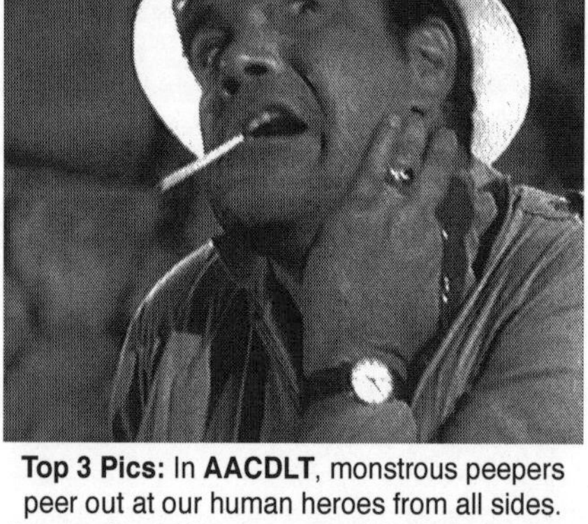

Top 3 Pics: In **AACDLT**, monstrous peepers peer out at our human heroes from all sides. **Above:** David Reynoso gets it in the neck from something you wouldn't wanna meet in the dark...or in broad daylight either, for that matter

of both the expedition and the movie's musical score. From the shadows, piercing, animalistic—but all-too-man-like—eyes observe the explorers' progress with far-from-impartial interest. Having discovered diamonds in the caves, the sole other female cast member, the self-serving and manipulative Prof. Laura character played by *señora* Domínguez, takes a flashlight and wanders off to explore in the darkness alone, whereupon she gets pounced upon by a large cyclopean beastie with a lizard-like tail in back ("That hideous monster!" shrieks a subtitle). More spurting blood results, but don't worry, it's just a flesh-wound. Following the attack, the sharp-eyed, quick-witted Prof. Díaz shrewdly deduces, "The size of that beast doesn't match the footprint we have". He theorizes that somehow within the complex network of caverns, evolution has for whatever reason become sidetracked, thus resulting in unknown species of animal ("strange creatures") which are disconnected from the main evolutionary chain (as in missing links). Later into the adventure, the cavers come across the ruins of an underground city, seen only in the distance (I was unsure if the long-shot of this hazy cityscape was a matte painting done specially for the present film, or simply yet another shot pinched from an existing production; if that latter quite likely possibility was indeed the case, I have no clue where the brief snippet of inserted footage originated). This plot development is soon thereafter abandoned, presumably for the simple reason that elaborating upon the idea would have greatly ratcheted-up costs on the production by necessitating the construction of special exterior/interior sets. So you can forget any lost subterranean civilization *à la* that seen in Virgil W. Vogel's **THE MOLE PEOPLE** (1956, USA), or a Pellucidar/Caprona-like underworld either, for that matter.

After Reynoso (co-star of Chano Urueta's *muy* mental **BLUE DEMON VS. THE INFERNAL BRAINS** [*Blue Demon contra los cerebros infernales*, 1966, Mexico; see *Monster! numero uno*, p.15]) bags one of the man-sized, one-eyed monsters with a knock-out cartridge from his hunting rifle, said creature keels over off a precipice to be skewered clear through on a sharp stalagmite, thus foiling their plans of capturing a live specimen. This flick's so cheap—not necessarily a liability, and definitely not in this case—that when one of the heroes levels and "shoots" his "machinegun" at the monster, we quickly realize that it's actually only a darn *rifle* he's shaking back and forth so convincingly, with "*Budda-budda-budda!*" noises dubbed over! You can tell they couldn't afford such costly luxuries as blanks either, because *zip*—absolutely *nada*—comes out of the muzzles of the firearms when they shoot them: no muzzle flash, no

A fuzzy long-shot of the upright-walking batzoid beastie, whose face doesn't even come close to matching-up with the makeup seen on the "same" creature during its close-ups (see bottom two stills on the next page)

nothing, just more economical sound FX are heard. All that amounts to mere nitpicking anyway in an endearingly primitive movie of this nature; so best you just sit back and enjoy all the dopey action and wrinkly-kneed monster costumes!

Evidently a tardy cash-in on the A-list 1959 *gringo* Jules Verne filmization **JOURNEY TO THE CENTER OF THE EARTH** (D: Henry Levin), at least this cut-price, modern-day-based variation *doesn't* contain the sickeningly saccharin Pat "Mr. Goody Two-Shoes" Boone—or any cutesy comic relief waterfowl, for that matter—and that's a definite major plus in **AVENTURA**'s favor, in my considered opinion! (But if I was forced to choose between Gertrude the duck and that buffoon Boone, I'd take the former option, thanks!) After a while, for all its mega-budget, spectacular sets and sprawling Cinemascope/Technicolor photography, **JOURNEY**'s optically-inflated pet lizards shot in an oversized terrarium grew a bit tiresome, too. Give me the present movie's remedial-level, poorly conceived dress-up critters anytime.

Amid all the elaborate and almost organic-looking geological strata while facing the constant threat of monstrous adversaries coming at them from out of the darkness on all sides, our cast being hot-blooded Latinos, romance and love triangles nonetheless still manage to blossom, with the boys outnumbering the girls at least three-to-one. In addition to all the other fun to be had here, it's fun sometimes too just spotting the crudely-muted spotlights employed to create "subtle" atmosphere and background ambience. With able assistance from prolific Mexploitation DP Raúl Martínez Soláres (who shot what sometimes seems to be virtually every Mexi-movie ever made, that's how often his name appears in their credits), German-born director Alfredo B. Crevenna ([1914-1996] still another super-prolific Mexploitationeer, whose credits are too numerous to mention) seems to be striving to instill an oppressively claustrophobic mood, but his efforts are rather thwarted somewhat by the spacious, all-too-authentic and well-lit cavern interior locations. Not that you'll be caring too much about atmospherics, what with that one-eyed monster ripping out secondary cast members' throats on a regular basis!

In a deep recess of the cave, our wounded cyclops is comforted by that big-clawed critter (which has still not been fully revealed, as yet) from the prologue, while Moreno's crew blasts and bashes

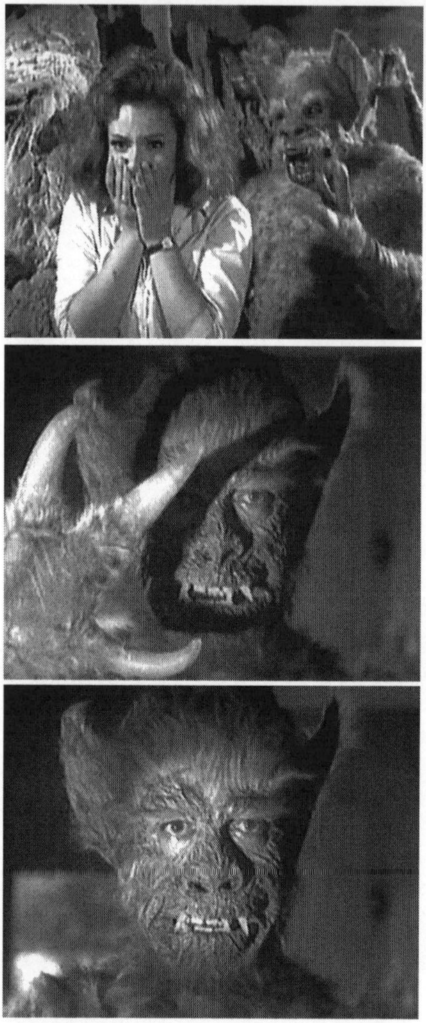

Top: Pretty Kitty de Hoyos is about to get carried away by a monster who is just bats about her in **AACDLT**. **Center & Above:** Believe it or not, these are C/U views of supposedly the same creature shown in the topmost shot and on the preceding page. But such things as poor continuity and mismatched shots only add to the film's endearing charm, in our expert opinion!

its way ever closer to the Earth's core. The usual river of molten magma presents an obstacle, so the men jerry-rig a line over the gorge and begin clambering across hand-over-hand while dangling from the rope slung between the two sides: in the process ideally setting themselves up for a massed air assault by floppy, elastic-stringed killer bats (XL specimens which may well have also seen use in more than one locally-shot vampire flick!). Of course, while being "dive-bombed" en masse by these yo-yoing creatures and trying to fend them off, one expendable explorer loses his grip on the lifeline and plummets to his fiery doom in the pulsing, pulpy mass of SFX oatmeal below.

Enraged at the demise of its inhuman buddy, the prologue-monster at last makes its full-frontal appearance; revealed to be a man-sized winged bat-thing. It (he? she?) promptly grabs one of the explorers and flies awkwardly off—interestingly enough, this development reminded me of a similar situation in the nifty '72 American TV flick **GARGOYLES**, as did other parts of **AACDLT**, too—then drops the victim to his death from a great height, rather like a seabird trying to crack open a shellfish by dropping it to the ground from the air (incidentally, certain other bits earlier in the action brought to mind moments from Jerry Jameson's **THE BAT PEOPLE** [1974, USA; see *M!* #8. p.26]). A war of wits is now waged between the trespassing humans and the revenge-bent bat-beast, who/which picks victims off one at a time in unexpectedly grisly fashion for the early/mid-'60s. We shortly take pause in the main narrative for an incidental subplot involving a wonderfully tacky scene wherein a treacherous thug shoves a rival into a ravine, where the man gets chomped and bloodied by the *papier mâché* mandibles of a giant spider that might well have scuttled (and quite possibly *did*) straight out of **QUEEN OF OUTER SPACE** or **WORLD WITHOUT END**! That same thug is then killed in turn by a vicious slash (—*¡SPURT!*—) of the bat monster's "razor sharp" rubber talons, and, by means of a handy waterlogged passage, it abducts the not unsurprisingly surprised heroine off to its lair, shades of a similar sequence at the climax of Jack Arnold's north-of-the-border aquatic critter classic **CREATURE FROM THE BLACK LAGOON** (1954).

Once again, **AACDLT**'s low budget rears its ugly head: in close-up, the monster possesses a distinctly different face than the one used for long-shots (even at that range, the dissimilarity is patently obvious in the extreme). These mismatched insert "reaction shots" of the more "human"-looking monster face, as opposed to the over-the-head mask seen on the long-shot suit, is admittedly an okay little makeup job—a kind of "werebat" variation of Lon Chaney, Jr.'s famous Jack P. Pierce Wolf Man look—although the mismatch between it and the more distant views of the whole monster is rather jarring, because they really don't look much alike at all, other than in the most rudimentary way. (I was reminded of *gringo* Edward Ludwig's classic shot-in-Mexico dimensional animation "big bug" flick **THE BLACK SCORPION** [1957], which employed a similar technique in depicting a wildly dissimilar monster whose C/U "shock insert" portraits didn't remotely match with the wider shots showing Willis H. O'Brien's titular stop-frame-animated critter. But such comparatively piddling continuity oversights spoil my enjoyment of neither that film nor this one, so I'll say no more about it.)

Events in **AVENTURA AL CENTRO DE LA TIERRA** wind to a close in predictably melodramatic fashion, but I won't give away the ending for the one or two of you out there who might feel inclined to track this movie down and see it for yourselves. I enjoyed it, but you can *tell* how easy to please *I am* when it comes to these crazy creepy-cheapies. Aw well, that's just me, I guess…

NOTE: A special "Thank You" goes out to my lovely co-ed Tim P. for kindly providing me with a fan-subbed copy of **AVENTURA** for review purposes here. It represented the first time I ever got to see the film in English, so it was truly a momentous occasion!

BREASTS & BEASTS

Interestingly enough—insert suitably pervy leer and snicker here!—**AVENTURA AL CENTRO DE LA TIERRA**'s lovely leading ladies Kitty de Hoyos (1941-1999) and Columba Domínguez (1929-2014) were numbered among the first actresses ever to appear (chastely, "artistically") nude on Mexican movie screens. According to acclaimed Mexican film historian Emilio García Riera's massive, multi-volume reference work *Historia documental del cine méxicano* (Universidad de Guadalajara, 1993), not only was 1955, historically speaking, the year that usage of both color film stock and Cinemascope cinematography were first introduced into Mexican-made motion pictures, but it was also a big year for cinematic skin, too. Both above-cited actresses would gain *mucho* mileage in the domestic press of the period for their undraped "cheesecake" appearances in a number of homegrown productions. Once controversial and even more than a little shocking to some (especially Vatican-appointed moral watchdogs), such scenes nowadays appear harmlessly innocuous in the extreme…but in those pre-Permissive Era days they were hot stuff indeed!

Columba Domínguez strikes an alluring pose in **LA VIRTUD DESNUDA** (1957)

Such "incidental" (i.e., commercially crucial) nudity was typically restricted to scenes which either involved exotically alluring, quasi-burlesque-style dance routines or, more commonly still, those wherein actresses revealed T&A (albeit never any actual pubic hair at this early stage, needless to say) as life models posing nude for some volcanically passionate male artist, typically in a hot-blooded Latin love story of the "*melodrama nudista*" variety. For instance, future several-time Mexi-monster movie heroine Ana Luisa Peluffo (born 1929)—who doffed her duds more frequently than many a Mexican actress did—played such a part in future **BRAINIAC** director Chano Urueta's romantic drama **EL SEDUCTOR** (*"The Seducer"*), and the same actress was cast as yet another nude life-study model in same director Urueta's **LA ILEGITIMA** (*"Illegitimate"*), both of which also originated in flesh-filled '55. More pseudo-*nudo* than all-out nude, although Peluffo's actual bare breasts were not revealed onscreen in the flesh, those in her photo-realistic painted portrait most certainly were—and were plentifully on display even as, oddly enough, her real ones were kept coyly out-of-frame.

Kitty de Hoyos in what may be a publicity pose for **ESPOSAS INFIELES** (1955)

Modeled (pun intended) along distinctly similar lines, Rosario Dúrcal—whose decidedly sparse filmography includes filling a supporting role in Federico Curiel's moody *Nostradamus* vampire serial (1960), starring Germán Robles in the title undead role—posed semi-nude for a painter in Miguel Morayta's **LAS MEDIAS DE SEDA** (*"Silk Stockings"*), also produced in that fateful, fleshful year of '55. (Incidentally, Morayta [1907-2013] was another director who subsequently made some memorable Mexi-monster movies, including **THE BLOODY VAMPIRE** [*El vampiro sangriento*, 1962] and its sequel **THE INVASION OF THE VAMPIRES** [*La invasión de los vampiros*, 1963], as well as the equally *fabuloso* **DOCTOR SATÁN** [1966].)

Although fleeting flashes of flesh had appeared in earlier decades in Mexican films (even as far back as the '30s), the mid-'50s saw a marked proliferation in onscreen skin as many more producers hurried to capitalize on the suddenly highly marketable trend. The aforementioned *señorita* Peluffo subsequently starred in Tito Davison's tame early "nudie" **LA DIANA CAZADORA** (*"Diana the Huntress"*, a.k.a. **CALL ME BAD**, 1956), whose cast included a whole bevy of other either *au naturel*-or-as-good-as *señoritas*, including Silvia Fournier, eventual heroine of Alfonso Corona Blake's wonderfully ambient **THE WORLD OF THE VAMPIRES** (*El mundo de los vampiros*, 1961). *¡Abiertamente revelamos!* (*"Openly exposed!"*) teased original posters for **DIANA**, which was yet another story about a nude model posing for an artist, this time a sculptor out to create a statue of the title character from Classical mythology. In one erotically-charged scene, Peluffo goes "all the way" by shedding her smokin' hot leopard-print bikini (the actress later starred in such primo Mexi-monster/horror fare as Rogelio A. González's **CONQUISTADOR DE LA LUNA** [*"Conqueror of the Moon"*, 1960] and Chano Urueta's **THE LIVING HEAD** [*La cabeza viviente*, 1963]).

Sparked by the mid-'50s T&A trend, similar "*desnudo artistico*" titillatory scenes as described above became commonplace in films of various genres. Her naughtiest naughty bits tastefully concealed by a sort of elaborate fig leaf G-string, **AVENTURA**'s future principal female lead de Hoyos bared almost all—if by no means everything—as essential set (un) dressing in José Díaz Morales' drama **ESPOSAS INFIELES** (*"Unfaithful Wives"*, 1955). As well as co-starring in Fernando Méndez's awesome monster/wrestling prototype **THE BODY SNATCHER** (*Ladrón de cadáveres*, 1957), **AVENTURA**'s future secondary lead actress Domínguez likewise did the nood thang upon occasion, including in Díaz Morales' **LA VIRTUD DESNUDA** (1957), another teasy adult-oriented drama which raised the censor's ire…and possibly other things besides (*wink*).

All this said, neither de Hoyos nor Domínguez get nekkid—or even anywhere close to it—in **AVENTURA AL CENTRO DE LA TIERRA** though, remaining fully-clothed throughout the runtime. While if they had stripped (*bonus!*) it might well have been an added selling point, the film's abundance of critters more than makes up for its severe shortage of titties. It wasn't until the late 1960s that breasts and beasts shared cinema screens in several "*horror y sexo*" adults-only titles. Directed by René Cardona, Sr., these were "straight" horror outings which were spiced-up with "explicit" nudie footage in alternate versions intended for release into more permissive foreign markets (such as over in Europe). ~ **Les Moore**

BONUS EXTRA COVER REVIEW!

SEÑOR STEVE'S MEXICAN SCI-FI DOUBLE-BILL!

by Stephen R. Bissette

Y'know, there are times when I weaken. I'll be watching a 1960s Italian SF movie, and I'll think, "Jeez, they *couldn't* have made any SF films lamer than this in the 1960s!"

Then I start to watch something like Alfredo B. Crevenna's **GIGANTES PLANETARIOS** (1967) and I realize how incredibly naïve and simple-minded I really am. But then I stay with it, and I realize I am not nearly as naïve and simple-minded as either these filmmakers were, or thought their audiences were, or—well—*both*.

Prof. Daniel Wolf (Guillermo Murray) ends up—hey, get this!—on a rocket ship with *three* stowaways—a moron boxer, his maladroit trainer, and Wolf's main squeeze—to land on Romania (yes, *Romania*), "the world of eternal night", to take out a pointy-headed megalomaniac warmonger Guardian/Protector (José Gálvez) on a world that looks like a Mexican *pepla* knockoff because…well, it *is*. Per the title, there *is* a planet. Putting lie to the title, there are *no* giant or giants, but there are doofy helmets (with antennae), togas, posing, treachery, dopey jokes (including a fat alien woman named "Bean"), and endless *yakyakyak* revolving around one-of-a-kind "plans" the Protector needs that Wolf has (hidden, at one point, under an antique desk with gum keeping it in place).

Crevenna made some fun stuff (my personal fave is the batmen-beneath-the-earth gem **AVENTURA AL CENTRO DE LA TIERRA**, 1965; see p.6), but as for this… give me **LA NAVE DE LOS MONSTRUOS** (1960) any day!

—

I thought Columbia's **VALLEY OF THE DRAGONS** (a.k.a. **PREHISTORIC VALLEY**, 1961, USA) was the last hurrah of that old **ONE MILLION B.C.** (1940, USA) lizards-as-dinosaurs foot-

age being used to create entirely new films around, but I was wrong!

Thanks to Tim Paxton, I've revisited Alfredo Salazar's and Rafael Portillo's confection **LA ISLA DE LOS DINOSAURIOS** (*"Island of the Dinosaurs"*, 1967) a couple times in all its glory, finally with English subtitles (I had seen it on VHS, but *sans* subtitles), and—*wow!*—what an anachronism this must have been in its own time!

When the subtitled version first fell into my talons, this marvelous caveman clunker made 80 minutes fly by while I had over a 100-degree fever, making this fever-dream undoubtedly more pleasurable than it has any right to be. Doubtless rushed out to cash in on Hammer's **ONE MILLION YEARS B.C.** (1966, UK) in the Mexican market, Salazar & Portillo weave a complete film out of new footage inserted carefully into **ONE MILLION B.C.** caveman and lizard/dino footage, along with clips from **NABONGA** (1944, USA) and a bit of Bert I. Gordon's **KING DINOSAUR** (1955, USA), changing costumes as necessary to ensure as seamless integration as was affordable.

Between Carole Landis' Loana and Raquel Welch's Loana, insert Alma Delia Fuentes as Laura, modern-day "mineralogist" who falls for caveman Molo (Armando Silvestre), in full Victor Mature/Tumak mode. Matriarchal Laura teaches Molo's tribe to revere Molo's mom, to love their children, and not to beat the living shit out of each other at dinner time, thanks to some Miss Manner's improvised flat-stone tableware and their first dose of etiquette.

The movie is quick as a shot getting its intrepid quartet of modern-day explorers to the "lost island" the Professor (Manuel Fábregas) speculates malingers in the Atlantic, uncharted and undiscovered; they're there in six minutes flat, but it takes a whole hour before any of them but Laura leave the camp long enough to see a single prehistoric monster.

In an early hilarious scene, Laura takes a piece of freshly-hammered-from-a-boulder rock and holds it over a Geiger counter-like device, which sets the meter needle rising, and she declares, "*Ah!* It's prehistoric!" It's geology like none practiced on this planet—except, perhaps, in the minds of low-budget filmmakers and Creationists. Ah, if only it had Lorena Velázquez as the female lead! Well, there *is* co-star Elsa Cárdenas as the chemist Esther; she dodges the **KING DINOSAUR** stock footage in the home stretch.

En route, yes, there are dinosaurs—thanks to Laura's wandering, all of 'em lifted from **ONE MILLION B.C.** and **KING DINOSAUR**—and Ray Corrigan's gorilla outfit (I'm pretty sure those are snipped from Sam Newfield's chestnut **NABONGA**), ill-matched with a real rat-bag of a gorilla suit (to supplant the Allosaurus attack footage in **ONE MILLION B.C.**). It's the most attentive recontextualization of **ONE MILLION B.C.** footage since W. Merle Connell's **UNTAMED WOMEN** (1952, USA), and that's a compliment in my bunker.

Dino-buffs, don't miss this one if you get the chance to see it; all other sane bipedal sentient beings, beware!

(©2012, 2015 Stephen R. Bissette, revised and expanded from an April 18, 2012 Facebook post.)

The **ONE MILLION B.C.** (1940) customized-with-a-rubber-horned-headpiece armadillo returned in **LA ISLA DE LOS DINOSAURIOS** ("Island of the Dinosaurs", 1967)—and still looked like an armadillo

Michael Mann's **The Keep***: An Appraisal*

by Dawn Dabell

In 1981, F. Paul Wilson released the novel *The Keep*, a wartime horror story set within an abandoned keep in a fictitious Romanian mountain pass. The book was the first instalment of what has since become known as *The Adversary Cycle*, and is still popular to this day. Fans of the original novel would no doubt have been excited when, just two years later, director Michael Mann adapted it for the screen, no doubt eagerly anticipating how Mann would present this interesting and atmospheric story on film. After experiencing the theatrical version, author Wilson was less than enthused by the director's interpretation of his novel (he declared the final product "a bad movie", and described watching it as "a very bitter experience"). Wilson felt that Mann had the ingredients at his disposal to make a film which should've been a critical success, but in his opinion it just didn't materialize.

Since the film's initial release, even the director himself has been less than glowing about how it turned out. Fans are constantly demanding a Director's Cut, but so far Mann has refused to open the vaults and release a more complete version, meaning that the 96 minutes currently available is as complete as it gets. What adds to the intrigue is that, over the years, the film has developed a cult status, and is one of those movies which endlessly divides people. Some find it a wholehearted disappointment, while others sing its praises at every given opportunity. But one has to wonder if those who are generally disappointed with it are people who read the book prior to viewing the film? There's certainly a lot more love for the book overall, though how much of a bearing this has over people's thoughts on the film is debatable. The critics certainly seem to agree with author Wilson, classing **THE KEEP** (1983, USA) as a bit of a misfire. Derek Winnert called the final piece "weird and confused, but this exotic war/horror brew is directed with lots of visual flair by Mann". Other critics went for an unsubtle play on words, coming up with gems like: "You can keep **THE KEEP**" and "Keep away from **THE KEEP**".

1986 Berkley Books paperback edition

The film has an intriguing plot. Nazi soldiers under the command of honorable and brave *Hauptmann* ("Captain") Woermann (Jürgen Prochnow), arrive at an ancient keep in the Carpathian Alps. The keep is located beside a small mountain village. Upon

German VHS box for **THE KEEP**

entering the building, the soldiers are warned by the locals that no one stays in the keep; the few travelers who have attempted to spend the night have fled out into the open, scared away by troubled dreams.

The keep is full of strange cross-like shapes on the walls, hundreds of them. Some soldiers believe the crosses are silver, but are told they are in fact worthless nickel and that they should not remove them. Later that night, a pair of opportunistic soldiers hack one out of the wall anyway…and are promptly killed by some unseen creature from behind the wall. It quickly becomes apparent that the keep was not built to keep attackers out—it was in fact built to keep something *in*. And that "something" has now been awakened!

In Greece, a mysterious man named Glaeken (Scott Glenn) senses that an old enemy has been set free, and urgently makes plans to set sail for Romania. Meanwhile, Nazi soldiers are being killed night after night, and Woermann is certain that whatever is killing his men is not of human origin. He requests relocation, but instead a team of ruthless SS Eisatzkommandos is sent in to sort out the problem, headed by the psychopathic Major Kaempffer (Gabriel Byrne).

Jewish professor Theodore Cuza (Ian McKellen) is brought in to offer his expertise on the history of the building, along with his vulnerable but spirited daughter Eva (Alberta Watson). Bit by bit, it becomes apparent that the creature which has been released is called Molasar, an ancient being from a long-forgotten past. Glaeken is Molasar's adversary—a Yin to his Yang—a being equally old and powerful who must face him in a final battle to the death.

When shooting wrapped on the movie, its running time came in at just over 3 hours, but much of it ended up on the cutting room floor. For whatever reason, the film was shorn of over half its original duration and was released at just over 90 minutes. It seems likely this was at Paramount's behest rather than Mann's. For a film based on a book in which so much happens, this final running time seems to be outrageously short. The studio no doubt had their reasons to call for such cuts, but it's obvious that many important scenes were chopped out as a result. Key aspects of the storyline are touched upon so briefly that if the viewer misses half a sentence or a minor gesture, they can end up hopelessly confused at what is going on later in the film. For example, the whole issue about Glaeken having no reflection and removing all

Ian McKellen as Dr. Cuza has a *tête-à-tête* with the keep's demonic denizen, the looming Molasar

the mirrors from his room at the inn is skimmed over so perfunctorily that it is actually easy to miss that it has any significance at all. Likewise, when Molasar explains about the talisman that needs to be taken out of the keep in order to free him, the line is delivered so fast and garbled that if you miss a word of it you will not know what McKellen is digging for and carrying to the exit near the end of the film. There are various other important points that are not explained, or explained only cursorily, to the audience. The ending of the theatrical print of **THE KEEP** seems remarkably sudden—there's the briefest of fights between the main adversaries: Molasar and Glaeken are sucked through the wall, seemingly dead; then Eva turns to look back towards the keep, and the end-credits begin to roll. That's *it*. Blink, sneeze, fart or cough…and you'll miss it! There is actually an extended alternate ending, which can be found on sites such as YouTube, in which Eva returns to the keep and goes down into the underground sub-cellar in search of Glaeken, believing he may have survived his conflict against Molasar. Earlier in the film, we have briefly been told that Glaeken only lives to defeat Molasar, that when one is destroyed it will probably destroy the other, too. In the extended ending, Eva finds Glaeken alive, now transformed into a mortal man with a reflection, and they are presumably free to live happily ever after, together!

In **THE KEEP**, Gabriel Byrne as SS Maj. Kaempffer comes to the realization that there is a greater evil even than the Nazis

Director Mann endows the film with a dreamlike quality, creating stunning visuals and an atmospheric feel. The scenes which feature Molasar are built up wonderfully, with swirling mist and dramatic electronic music, leaving the audience tense, hungrily anticipating what will happen next. Although the film is seen as a horror movie, very little blood or gore is actually seen onscreen other than during the first attack on the soldiers who disturb Molasar's tomb. The scares are mainly created through build-up—it's more about messing with the *mind* of the viewer rather than anything actually seen onscreen. The set design and locations are superb, with a lusciously green Welsh quarry standing in for the Romanian locale of the story. The keep itself looks dramatic and imposing, a towering and ominous-looking wall leading to a maze of dingy corridors and eerie chambers.

The monster of the film is some kind of alien-like force which gradually grows from a mist-shrouded, skeletal being with ligaments on show to some-

Scott Glenn as Glaeken and the recently late Alberta Watson (1955-2015) as Eva are part of eerie goings-on at the creepy keep of the title

Makeup technician Beryl Lerman adds some details to the Molasar character (played by Michael Carter)

thing strong and powerful-looking as he feeds off all the death and fear around him. The monster of the book is more of a tall, vampiric figure, a robed giant with long hair and a foul presence. That too would have worked in the film, though the mountainous creature created here remains an impressive enough movie monster. In '80s cult cinema, Molasar has become something of a minor icon.

Many people disagree about the value of the soundtrack by German electronic group Tangerine Dream. Some love the score and believe it to be one of the key successes in the film; others find it completely wrong and go so far as to say it ruins the overall feel and effectiveness of the production. Whether you love or hate the effect it creates, there is no denying that Tangerine Dream had real longevity in the film business, scoring films such as **SORCERER** (1977), **RISKY BUSINESS** (1983, both USA), **SPASMS** (1983, Canada), **FIRESTARTER** (1984, USA), **LEGEND** (1985, USA/UK), **NEAR DARK** (1987) and **RED HEAT** (1988, both USA). Prior to working on **THE KEEP**, Tangerine Dream collaborated with Michael Mann on his debut production, **THIEF** (1981, USA). The soundtrack for **THE KEEP** is very much of its era, similar in some ways to the sword-and-sorcery scores of the same decade. Personally, I feel that it adds to the atmosphere of the final feature: the thunderous electronic strains help to create excitement in the viewer where needed, and build tension at key moments. The score is sometimes used to eliminate the need for dialogue; often the story is told as much through its music as through the words the characters are speaking.

Although in retrospect **THE KEEP** was deemed a theatrical flop, at the time of release it seems Paramount had high hopes for it—they endorsed a lot of spin-off merchandise alongside companies like Mayfair Games. For example, the company manufactured a board game based on the movie which allows players to participate as either Molasar or Glaeken, and the aim of the game is to find the talisman (the sword's hilt) which is located at the centre of the keep. These days, the game isn't easy to come by, and for anyone determined enough to track it down it can be a little pricey. Fans of the film will no doubt find it a fun way to while away an afternoon with equally avid **KEEP** fans. Mayfair Games also released an RPG (Role Playing Game) based on the film to appeal to fans of RPGs such as *Dungeons & Dragons*.

In recent years, F. Paul Wilson scripted a 5-part comic series telling the story of **THE KEEP**, with artwork provided by artist Mathew Smith (Smith is most widely known for his work on the comic *Hellboy*). These were later turned into a graphic novel, complete with a foreword by Wilson in which he explains to the reader why he chose to adapt his book into this format, especially since the reception of the film adaptation was so negative. In his opening lines he states, "If not for a bad movie, I might have let someone else do this". This foreword seriously hammers home the fact that Wilson was left burned and scarred by what Mann did to his novel. He makes it very clear that his aim in approving the graphic novel, and scripting the worded parts of it himself, was to ensure *this* version was true to his original story. He also goes on to explain: "I consider this visual presentation of **THE KEEP** my version of the movie, what could have been...what should have been". It's certainly a fun version of the story, featuring some wonderful illustrations and, for the fans, it's a worthy addition to their collection. It could almost be viewed as a storyboard for the film that Wilson wishes they'd actually made of his book. It must be noted, however, that for people not familiar with the book, the graphic novel is quite confusing in parts.

Fans of **THE KEEP** will also be happy to hear that a "making-of" documentary entitled **A WORLD WAR II FAIRYTALE: THE MAKING OF MICHAEL MANN'S THE KEEP** is due out in 2016 according to the IMDb. Hopefully this will come to fruition.

Fans of the book will certainly find the film worth watching, although many may come away feeling that the book is far better than Mann's adaptation. Maybe a longer cut with some of the missing footage restored might make for a more satisfying overall experience? **THE KEEP** does have a strong following, and fans are still hungry for a DVD or Blu-ray release. Having read—and loved—the book, I think the film adaptation is a missed opportunity. It is intriguing, interesting and visually fine, but I expected more, and the 96-minute version most commonly seen just doesn't quite deliver it. Maybe one day a fuller version might come to light? *Here's hoping!*

REVIEWS

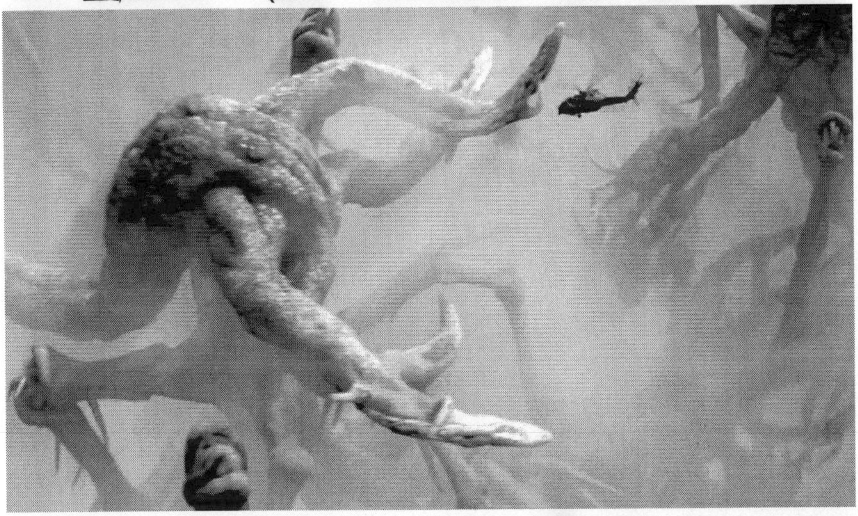

The gargantuan free-ranging extraterrestrial organisms of **MONSTERS: DARK CONTINENT** are a truly awe-inspiring sight to behold!

MONSTERS: DARK CONTINENT

Reviewed by Brian Harris

UK, 2014. D: Tom Green

Back in 2010, filmmaker Gareth Edwards directed an engaging science fiction drama entitled **MONSTERS**, which attained quite a bit of critical success and quickly became a "thinking man's" fan favorite. The film, set 6 years after an alien invasion, is really more of a romance/road trip/buddy film/drama in which a journalist and his editor's daughter fall in love, while he attempts to usher her safely through the "Infected Zone", a border between Mexico and the United States populated by alien behemoths. The film was different—not at all the kind of science fiction fans were expecting to see, especially with a title like **MONSTERS**—and the difference was the "human experience". Science fiction has typically mainly focused on technology (e.g., mind-control devices, spacecraft, robots, laser guns, etc.), but films like Steven Soderbergh's **SOLARIS** (2002, USA), Danny Boyle's **SUNSHINE** (2007, UK/USA), Duncan Jones' **MOON** (2009, UK), John Hillcoat's **THE ROAD** (2009, USA), Benedek Fliegauf's **WOMB** (2010, Germany/Hungary/France), Mike Cahill's **ANOTHER EARTH** (2011, USA), and Bong Joon Ho's **SNOWPIERCER** (2013, South Korea/Czech Republic/USA/France) all reinvigorated the oft-neglected human element. It was always there, of course, but it was constantly being buried under layers of *Star Wars* machine grease, *Star Trek* quasi-scientific tech lingo and *Matrix* razzle-dazzle. **MONSTERS** stripped it all down, made the antagonists almost an afterthought and brought two unlikely people together. I liked the film. It was inventive and beautiful to look at—and the monster aliens were breathtaking. But the very humanity that made **MONSTERS** so different was ultimately what turned me off as well; I wanted *more* monsters and *less* blossoming romance. I'm such a heel! In any event, I didn't like it enough to rush out and purchase it. That will change though if **MONSTERS: DARK CONTINENT** happens to be paired-up with it for a Blu-ray set.

When it was announced there would be a follow-up to **MONSTERS**—without Edwards at the helm—I think a lot of people were skeptical. And rightfully so. What he accomplished was admirable, and many were hoping the next film would maintain the spirit of the first, while also moving the concept forward. All it would take is a direc-

"SHOCKING. DISORIENTING. UNCONVENTIONAL. DISTINCTIVE"
★★★★
"THE HURT LOCKER' MEETS 'CLOVERFIELD'. AN ABSOLUTE MUST-SEE"
★★★★★
MONSTERS
DARK CONTINENT
FEAR HAS EVOLVED

tor or writer that didn't "get it" and the monsters would end up the focus, leaving humanity buried under so much so-so CGI. While I wasn't bowled over by **MONSTERS**, it's hard to deny Edwards' unique approach. Thankfully, director Tom Green (*Misfits*, 2009-10, USA) and his co-writer Jay Basu (**THE DINOSAUR PROJECT**, 2012, UK) were able to create a story that honors the first—keeping the aliens somewhat an afterthought—while also making it their own.

The events in **MONSTERS: DARK CONTINENT** take place 10 years after the first film and, much to America's chagrin, "infected zones" (IZs) have popped-up all over the world, threatening some of the nation's valuable foreign assets. When we first meet the film's protagonist Michael (Sam Keeley), he's part of a tightknit group of street kids from Detroit, preparing to say goodbye to their civilian lives and go kill monsters overseas. Of course, once there, they quickly realize their real job is to keep one another alive while reporting on monster herd positions and weeding-out insurgents. Tired of losing their family members to US air strikes on the monster herds, the insurgents set IEDs (improvised explosive devices) to combat intrusions by both monsters and soldiers.

One of the wee alien larvae from **MONSTERS: DARK CONTINENT** is about to undergo a startling metamorphosis

Led by team leaders Staff Sergeants Frater (Johnny Harris of *The Fades*, 2011, UK) and Forest, the team are called upon to enter deep into the "IZ" on a search and rescue. En route, an IED derails the mission, injuring one of the team and attracting the attention of local insurgents. Pinned down by gunfire, they're forced to retreat to an abandoned building to regroup and care for the wounded. One by one the team fall, leaving only Michael, his close friend Frankie and Staff Sgt. Frater alive. Though battered, bruised and taken hostage by insurgents, Frater insists the mission must be seen through to completion.

If the desert doesn't kill them first, the monsters, insurgents and insanity will!

In my opinion, **MONSTERS: DARK CONTINENT** was—prepare yourselves now—better than Edwards' film by leaps and bounds. Some of you Edwards/**GODZILLA** (2014, USA/Japan) fanboys are probably cursing my name right now: fair enough. The first had the whole "romance/road trip/buddy film/drama" thing going for it; this was more along the lines of a "coming of age/buddy film/war drama" (with aliens, of course). It was gritty, brave and offensive; everything you'd expect to see in a film about war. The dialogue has just the right amount of he-man swagger, the actors are solid and, of course, the aliens we do get look outstanding. It only makes sense that a film which focuses more attention on characters than CGI can afford a bit more quality on the brief money shots. Viewers will not be disappointed with the monsters in this, that's a promise. Hell, Green & Co. even give us some monster variants, as well as glimpses into the mourning behavior and spawning habits of the aliens. Truly fascinating! We'll likely discover more about these creatures in the next film, and I have no doubt there will be another.

While I can't say all war films have subtext, many do. Whether they speak against the evils of war or the greater "good" of fighting for peace, war films often try to relay some kind of message. Viewers

No Man's Land: In the still-ongoing *Monsters* movie franchise, massive tentacled beasties roam free over the Earth, and must (hopefully) remain contained within segregated "Infected Zones". Thing is, it's in a monster's nature not to do what it's told…and therein lies the problem!

may expect some here, but I'll leave it up to you all to come away from the film with whatever you will. I can say this: it's no coincidence that Michael finds himself depending so heavily on Johnny Harris' character Sgt. Noah Frater, a deeply affected man, to get him through his mission. I don't mean to be "that guy", but with a first name like Noah—a rather well-known Biblical figure with a higher calling—and the surname Frater—the Latin meaning of which is "brother"—you quickly catch on that writers Green and Basu did indeed have "something" to say.

I was close to proclaiming this a good film and a decent sequel, until a few tears found their way from my eyes. **MONSTERS: DARK CONTINENT** is a superior film to the first and it's incredibly moving, and in many ways beautiful. The sand, the monsters, the pain; it has all the trappings of something that deserves a well-earned run in theaters. There's currently no release date set yet, but this film is still available for streaming rental on Amazon, which I'd highly recommend to science fiction fans looking for something unique. I really hate poster quotes that feature the whole "SUCH-AND-SUCH MOVIE MEETS SUCH-AND-SUCH MOVIE", as they often oversimplify a film to the point of turning me off, but I'd say in this case Final Reel's quote, **"THE HURT LOCKER** Meets **CLOVERFIELD"** was accurate. If that sounds intriguing to you, please do check it out. I, for one, cannot wait until I get this on Blu-ray.

WIZARDS OF THE LOST KINGDOM

(*El mago del reino perdido*, a.k.a. **WIZARD WARS** [working title])

Reviewed by Adam Parker-Edmondston

Argentina/USA, 1985. D: Héctor Olivera

Monster movies can be found far and wide. From the mainstream movies made by the Hollywood studios, straight through down to the bargain-basement movies you might find in your local video store's discount bin, to the streaming horrors found on various movie channels, we creature feature fans are spoiled rotten for choice. There is one avenue of entertainment which I have not yet mentioned that can give monster movie fans a bit of a buzz, but it takes a bit of work: I'm talking about movies on VHS. If lucky, a VHS collector can dig through discount bins and find features that have never (and probably never will) get released on disc. This is where I came across an extraordinarily enchanting fantasy movie, crammed to the gills with odd creatures, monsters and a whole heap of tat thrown in for good measure. **WIZARDS OF THE LOST KINGDOM** is that movie, and once seen it can *never* be unseen!

In the film's prologue sequence that rips huge chunks out of the cheapo sword-and-sorcery adven-

WIZARDS OF THE LOST KINGDOM's Thom Christopher is better-known as Hawk on TV's *Buck Rogers in the 25th Century*

ture **DEATHSTALKER** (1983, Argentina/USA, D: "John Watson"/James Sbardellati)—which it does frequently—we are introduced to a fantasy world full of magic, exotic kingdoms, assorted royalty and subterfuge/betrayal. The film drops us straight in the deep end as we are introduced to the major annoyance that goes by the name of Prince Simon (Vidal Peterson). Wanting to impress the princess, he decides to bust out his magic mojo by bringing a gargoyle to life. In a piece of unintended grotesqueness, the poor gargoyle cannot move, as his feet are stuck to the ground, and it resultantly makes a horribly pitiful whining sound like a small child. Then the poor thing is never heard from again! This is kind of messed-up, and I have seen less horrific things in a David Lynch movie…but this one is PG-rated, FFS! What we can gather from this is that magic is pretty much a throwaway commodity in this kingdom. So is dry ice, which we see *all over* the damn kingdom, especially in the wizard's inner sanctum. Nothing makes a cauldron more believable than oodles of dry ice! The film also, very handily, color-codes the magic which the wizards use; so, blue is good and red is bad (hey, it worked for **STAR WARS**!). Throw in a small bat-monster lackey (the credits actually list it as "Bat Creature") and your introduction to the wondrous kingdom is complete. All of this happens in the first 15 minutes, so don't be worrying about pacing issues; this movie has far too much to show you in a short space of time to waste any of it on playing the long game.

As we march on through this low-budget piece of awesomeness, we see a magical kingdom come under threat from a once-trusted magician but now all-'round bad dude Shurka (played by "I think I remember that guy's face from something or other" Thom Christopher, who is better known to some for playing the alien birdman Hawk on the TV series *Buck Rogers in the 25th Century* [1979-81]). In **WIZARDS**, Shurka has teamed up with the Queen to rid themselves of King Tylor (Augusto Larreta) and take over the kingdom…which he does in a mere matter of *seconds*. Disturbingly, Shurka seems to have strange designs on the princess, who is quite obviously underage (this seems to be a bit of running theme, as elsewhere a grown woman attempts to seduce the juvenile Simon in the forest). As you would expect, being as he is the main villain, Shurka is a total dick. He derives great pleasure from disintegrating his vertically-challenged minions, and also likes to shout out his lines in a weird, inaudible drivel which is pretty funny to listen to; not so helpful when it comes to plot exposition, though. Luckily, the film has very little plot to worry about anyway.

There is so much to love about this movie! Just look at the characters involved: We have Simon, the young wannabe magician who is on the run from Shurka's men and who is the holder (and the loser) of a magical ring; and Kor the conqueror, played by Bo Svenson ("played" is perhaps too much of a compliment here, as he really phones-in this performance). Kor evidently thinks he is the sword-and-sorcery genre's version of Han Solo, but he plays it so half-arsed and lazily you'll wonder if he's even awake in half of his scenes. One of his first lines of dialogue is, "Do you have any wine?" Can't fault a guy for trying, I guess. Even though Kor acts like a jerk, you just know he is going to help the kid out, or else the movie would be over pretty quickly. Seriously: Simon is *useless*! "Simple" doesn't quite cover it. He drops the magical ring almost immediately after being told to keep it (because it contains all of the wizard's concentrated power). Luckily, Simon's dad uses his wizard-like powers to talk to Simon much like a Jedi would. But only for one scene.

This motley band of misfits go off on a magical adventure; which is when the film really comes into its own. After stabbing some dude to death, Simon gets captured by a group of evil female witches. This leads to an amazing scene involving a huge flying beast, which is almost certainly taken from another movie (though I cannot for the life of me remember which film it steals from)! *[It's from Jack Hill's **SORCERESS** (1982, USA/Mexico) –ed.]* They then save a vertically-challenged wizard's house from being ransacked by goblins. This film must have had the same handful of actors on call 24/7, because these vertically-challenged people pop up all over the place! Just for a change of pace they then nip into a cave to fight ghosts and a very small dragon, which luckily likes to eat bats more than humans. After Tor narrowly avoids marrying a cyclops, we are well on our way to the end, which involves a mermaid making a rainbow bridge in order for our heroes to get to the castle. This leads to one of my favorite lines, where the mermaid says to Tor, "I have tested your manhood". I'm sure you have, but this is children's picture, so let's keep it clean, shall we! The beauty of this movie is you just take all of this zaniness in your stride when you watch it; it just seems to fit, because the team behind this movie throw everything but the kitchen sink into it! We lead up to the final confrontation at the castle, where Tor and Simon must sort Shurka out once and for all. You will be happy to know most of this ending is stolen from the aforementioned first *Deathstalker* movie. Simon does get to throw down some magical lightning bolts in one of the only original scenes shot for the ending, so if you really want to see him get to let loose, this is the scene for you.

WOTLK is one of those films where they're desperate for the lead to grow into the hero they all need him to be, but Simon is so devoid of any onscreen charisma whatsoever that he basically just *sucks*, so you don't really care much about him either way. What you do care about is the incredibly cheesy assortment of monsters the film throws into its cinematic mix.

Now, I have mentioned a few of the creatures on show here already, but I wanted to go into a bit more detail on some of my favorites. The best by far is Simon's pet. Named Gulfax, it's really just Chewbacca in an oversized white doggy outfit, which is so loose-fitting you can see the gaps. Only Simon can understand him/it, and he/it speaks in nothing but random gibberish. He/it is not in the movie enough for my liking! The Spider People are an interesting creation, too. Essentially huge rubbery spiders, which—even though they look naff—terrified me. They have a confrontation in a cave with Simon after they have tried to seduce him in their female forms (a similar scene happens in the great monster movie **SPOOKIES** (1986, USA/Netherlands [see *Monster!* #13, p.41 and *Weng's Chop* #7, p.157]). There are zombies—which actually look pretty good, to be fair—that Simon brings back for no real reason (yeah, the kid learnt necromancy pretty quickly!), and they quote **THE EVIL DEAD** by saying "*Join us!*" constantly. These poor undead corpses are those of slain warriors whom Simon thought it would be a good idea to have a chat with. They do not share the same sentiment, and fancy knocking him off, but they wind up getting re-killed instead. Which is good for them, as that's pretty much what they wanted anyway!

Top: Bo Svenson slums it as Kor the wandering warrior in **WOTLK**; accompanying him is his shaggy, sheepdog-like sidekick, Gulfax (Edgardo Moreira). **Center:** The film's flyin' lion. **Above:** '80s US VHS cover

UK VHS cover

Elsewhere, there are also some lizard men that look like they just walked in from **DEATHSTALKER**, and they are great fun to behold. We first see these creatures teasing a gnome who is also a wizard and a hobgoblin (?). I lost track a bit here, but watching these creatures bossing around a vertically-challenged chap is oddly enough not the oddest thing you will see in this movie. They decide to bring in a bigger colleague, who does about as well as they did in teasing said hobgoblin/gnome/wizard. We subsequently bump into a painfully false-looking bat and what I can only assume is a dragon in a cave, but it looks a heck of a lot more like a rejected Muppet to me. We then get to some truly bizarre stuff involving a gang of tusked cyclopses who can't make up their minds whether they want to eat our group or get married to them. There is also a strange guy with a frog-like head (I have *no idea* what he is meant to be doing in this movie!); maybe not what you would see in children's movies today, but bless 'em for trying to appeal to all. Now, no matter what I have said about these creatures in this review, let me make myself clear: I absolutely *love* them! The film tries so hard to bring us this collection of fantastical beasts, which is obviously a major hindrance when you only have a budget of a few quid. But I love the fact that they tried to create these creatures from scratch (or else nicked them from other movies), and it is this menagerie of crazy creatures which truly makes the film that little bit extra-special. Well, that and the awful acting, stolen scenes from other movies, bad plot points, etc., etc.

As if all this wasn't enough to get you wanting to watch it, just wait until you see the UK VHS cover for **WOTLK**, which is very interesting. Like I mentioned in my **SNAKEMAN** (2005, Canada/USA) review last issue (#15, p.51), it seems that film distributors can get away with murder when it comes to misleading covers. At least that for **WOTLK** does attempt to give us a decent interpretation of what the film has in store for us. It depicts a majestic castle, but its onscreen counterpart inspires little awe and is really only seen at the end (it looks very wobbly and is nowhere near water, unlike the one on the cover). The cover's **THE DARK CRYSTAL**-styled monster in reality onscreen looks more like something from "Drake Floyd"/Claudio Fragasso's **TROLL 2** (1990, Italy/USA), and the amazing flyin' lion Simon is shown riding on the box appears in the movie for two minutes (tops) and looks more like a steroid-shooting Lion-O rip-off with wonky wings. The cover artist even messed Simon's appearance up, as he is clearly an adult in the artwork, and not only that but blond to boot. In the film he is black-haired: on the cover he looks like Luke Skywalker! This flick is truly on the level of **TROLL 2** for just plain awfulness and ironic entertainment value. Everything about it is terrible, from the acting, the stolen sets with their mismatched dressings, to the ropy dialogue, the tawdry wardrobe and disjointed plot, which bounces from one set-piece to another with no real rhyme or reason. And the Kingdom is not even really "lost" at all; it has merely been taken over!

This movie looks and feels like a '80s movie in every sense of the word. It oozes strange beasts, generic storytelling, innocence and naïvety mixed with some dark undertones, as well as a sense of wonderment and excitement. What it does is mix all these wonderful things together to create this incredibly bad, yet hugely entertaining movie. I love bad movies, but as I have said before there is a knack to getting them right. This bangs it straight on the head! Much like **FLIGHT TO HELL** (*Volo per l'inferno*, 2003, Italy), which I covered a couple of issues back (#14, p.64), this is a film that never gets mentioned on any so-bad-they're-great lists. Hopefully, this review will help change that!

NOTE: The sequel was Charles B. Griffith's **WIZARDS OF THE LOST KINGDOM II** (1989, USA), co-starring David Carradine, Lana Clarkson, Mel Welles, Sid Haig and Henry Brandon.

DON'T BE AFRAID OF THE DARK

Reviewed by Eric Messina

USA, 1973. D: John Newland

The original version from 1973 traumatized me as a child. I had fuzzy memories of the demons featured here, with their gruesome prune-faces and sunken-in eyes. In the '70s there was an onslaught of terrifying made-for-TV films like this one, including **BAD RONALD** (1974), **DEVIL DOG: THE HOUND OF HELL** (1978) and **TRILOGY OF TERROR** (1975, all USA). It's as if some network executive greenlit all these harrowing films to send the youth of America straight into mental institutions or constant therapy to scrub those images from our collective consciousness. I remember looking into vents in my house to see if there might be a pair of eyeballs staring back at me from behind the walls, whispering my name as the little goblins did in the film to the main character, Sally. For years I would wonder, "What the hell was that movie that scared the shit out of me at such a young age?" and would it hold up if I revisited it? Thanks to Warner Archives, a pristine copy is now available for you to relive all your nightmares on DVD. The Guillermo Del Toro-produced remake can't hold a candle to the original version, even with its outdated polyester hokiness and thinly-disguised lesbian ambiguity (which gives it more depth, in my opinion). Everything about this movie stirs up Halloween-drenched imagery for me, from the opening shot of the eerily-lit house to the frightening double-tracked, echoey demonic voices that cry, "When will she set us free?!" What the *hell* are they talking about? Just the sound of these creatures raises the hairs on the back of my neck!

Whew, good thing they don't stick around in the daylight (or *do* they)? Kim Darby—an actress I know best as the mother in **BETTER OFF DEAD** (1985, USA)—plays Sally Farnham, who can't cook and on top of it has just moved into the house filled with supreme evil. Darby's hair looks like it's eating her face, and she comes off like a very butch lesbian (more on *that* ambiguousness later!). Mr. Harris, played by William Demarest, better known as Uncle Charlie from *My Three Sons* (1960-73, USA), is the handyman who refuses to unbolt the basement fireplace. Sally is just asking for trouble, and gleefully cracks open all the nuts and bolts securing the pits of hell that are just beneath the fireplace aching to be set free. The marriage between Sally and Alex (played by Jim Hutton, who was subsequently seen in Ray Danton's astral projection shocker **PSYCHIC KILLER** [1975, USA]) seems horrible; she's treated like his domestic servant, and they seem to hate each other. At first

The prune-headed, diminutive-but-deadly whispering hobgoblins in **DON'T BE AFRAID OF THE DARK** really get under Kim Darby's skin—and *ours* too!

Fan art by Patrick J. McQuade

they think all the rustling and chewing going on is a rat problem instead of a demonic gnome infestation. The critters incessantly call her name and can't wait to kill her—I mean, they are overjoyed by the idea.

Sally and her blonde girlfriend look and dress like each other in a '70s business lesbian-style of dress, and they talk about Women's Lib as if it just came out last week. I think they make a better couple than Sally and Alex! Her happiness with Joan (played by Barbara Anderson) could be real if only her stupid husband would stay away indefinitely on one of his business trips. There's a certain amount of inappropriate sexual politics in this film (I guess in 1973 it was a hot-button issue; there was also a writer's strike going on during this production). Sally takes Uncle Charlie's approach in keeping the hellish beings from escaping by putting the screws back in the furnace, as "Oh, I'm just a stubborn woman, I should be allowed to do what I want", and the whole vibe is off-putting. Never mind that curt bullshit, because the über-creepy trolls have escaped and want to scare the shit out of Sally. The look of the monsters has a demented *H.R. Pufinstuf* (1969-70, USA) or Sid & Marty Krofft quality, which I think is brilliant. Michael Hancock—who worked on **THE OMEGA MAN** (1971 [see *Monster!* #13, p.76]), **DAY OF THE LOCUST** (1975) and **DEADLY FRIEND** (1986, all USA)—designed the ghoulish creatures, who look like they're distance cousins to the furry-bodied, pig-faced "man on the wing of the plane" from the famous "Nightmare at 20,000 feet" episode of *Twilight Zone* (1959-64, USA). They have gaunt, elongated features and bodies that resemble nasty leaves you'd find in gutters covered in rancid filth.

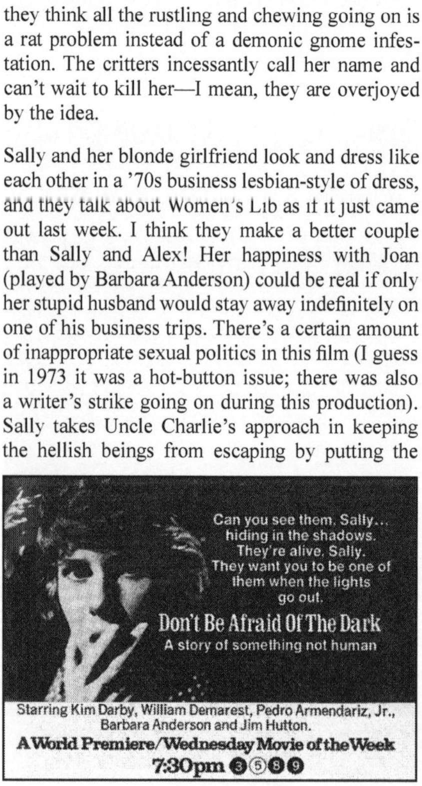

'73 *TV Guide* ad

Acting in the roles of the evil, whispering creatures were two famous little people, Tamara "**E.T.**" De Treaux and Felix Silla (whose many SF/monster/fantasy film credits include playing Misquamacus in William Girdler's **THE MANITOU** [1978, USA]).

At a fancy dinner party, Sally is nervous that the little demons will grab her dress and cause her to lose her shit in front of her high-class friends and embarrass her husband. The dinner party sequence couldn't be more ridiculous, with classical music playing and candlelight throughout the house. It's almost Douglas Sirk-esque in its over-the-top gaudy cluelessness.

Sally hearing voices and being haunted right out of her marriage could be a metaphor for a woman stressed-out from the pressures of her "straight partnership" in a loveless marriage.

There's no backstory as to why the hideous monsters specifically want to murder this woman, which makes it that much scarier. It's all shrouded in ambiguity and mythology (toward the end, as she joins them in whatever ghostly dimension wherein they reside, her voice joins theirs in the chorus of the damned). They need her soul for some unknown reason; there's no closure, which makes it all the more horrific.

I love the forced perspective of little people holding giant straight razors peeking from behind giant books, and their methods of scaring the shit out of Sally by standing on each other's shoulders to turn the light on. They're eerily hilarious! I'd welcome mice over these goblins with an insatiable bloodlust any day. I mean, *why* do they want to kill her anyway? It seems as if it's her own paranoia manifesting itself in the form of demons. One of my favorite moments is when the goblins accuse the handyman of being a snitch and cackle as they slash him with a razor and chant, "*You told! You told!*" It only happens for a minute but is nightmarish and a good example of what you can achieve with some creepy lighting and suitably evil-sounding voices. My mom and I used to whisper "Sally, we're coming to get you" at each other. I read somewhere that Guillermo Del Toro used to do the same thing, so this TV movie obviously affected a lot of people, and still holds up well today with its high levels of spookiness, even though it gets sort of eclipsed by the whole cheesy, drab polyester vibe.

Of course Sally's blonde friend Joan is the only one who believes that supernatural elements are causing her to have a mental breakdown and thinks coffee will solve everything (sometimes it does!).

The trolls turn her house into a pitch black death trap (locking all the doors) and continue to rhythmically chant her name over and over again as she moves through the dark house with a candle. She basically gives up and doesn't even try to grasp a hold of anything as they pull her with ropes down the stairs. It actually seems like she *wants* to die. They behave like Morlocks or Gremlins and are scared by flash photography, and, even after all her feeble attempts to survive through this goblin invasion, they still manage to plunge her into the depths of the fireplace. She ends up in their purgatory, from which they constantly wish to be set free, and the film drifts off without any explanation or comfort…

I *love* this film! It remains oddly fascinating and super-creepy.

ALIEN SIEGE

Reviewed by Christos Mouroukis

USA, 2005. D: Robert Stadd

Ad-line: *"They Were Asked To Die For The Good of Humanity. They Chose To Fight For Freedom Instead".*

Okay, Kulkus—in case you didn't know—are an alien race. Their breed is actually dying, and because there is no Greenpeace in space, I guess they decided to pay Earth a visit in order to avoid their annihilation. The problem is that the antidote to their disease is human blood. So they invade USA in order to fulfil their newfound lust.

All of the above sounds very cute, and as a matter of fact very **PLANET OF THE VAMPIRES**

(*Terrore nello spazio*, 1965, Italy/Spain)- or **LIFEFORCE** (1985, UK/USA)-like, but do bear in mind that Mario Bava this is not—not even *remotely*!—nor is it even Tobe Hooper. What's more, the film doesn't even focus on the elements above but on some character development instead. Said characters are Dr. Stephen Chase (Brad Johnson from **WILD THINGS: DIAMONDS IN THE ROUGH** [2005, USA]) who is the good guy and he is trying to protect his daughter (Erin Ross from **AVALANCHE SHARKS** [2013, Canada]) from the (not surprisingly) corrupt army officials.

The unfortunate thing in this film is the monsters. I mean, when your working title is **ALIEN BLOOD** you may not expect to see too much blood because you probably caught this flick on its SyFy broadcast, but you certainly expect some ugly motherfuckin' aliens, right? You want aliens even if they're going to look like Z-grade CGI, right? Well, you'll get aliens, but the problem is that they look like…*humans*. Yes, we the monster-loving audience are expected to buy mere *actors* "acting" as aliens. I felt ripped-off, to say the least!

What you should be tuning in for are the spaceship attacks, as the scenes in which they bombard our dear Earth are nothing less than spectacular. These CG FX may not be perfect, but they are not bad either, although I'm not sure if you can forgive too many things from a film that is bearing Universal Pictures' logo at the beginning, even when you know that it was actually only distributed by this major studio.

It was produced by Jeffery Beach (a veteran with almost a hundred genre films under his belt, main-

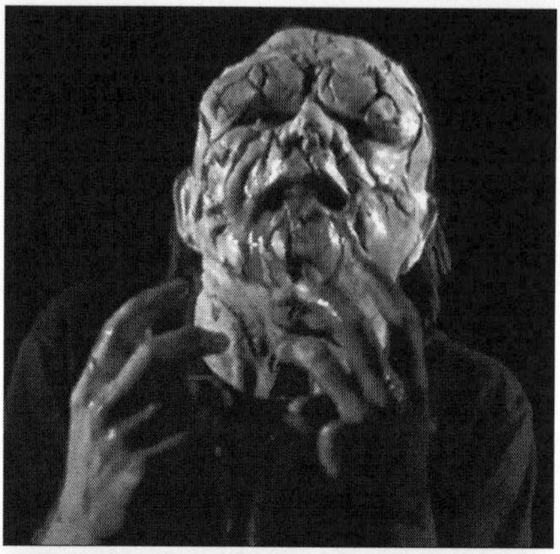

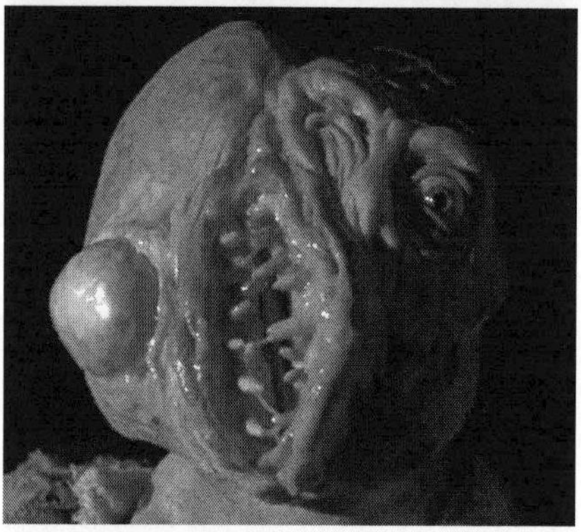

Top: In **BREEDERS**, makeup effects tech/actor Ed French plays a character who, c/o of cheapo-zoid bladder FX, transforms into a big bug. **Above:** Another **BREEDERS** beastie, whose mouth looks like a you-know-what with teeth

ly from the '00s; including my personal favorites, **LAKE PLACID 2** [2007], **LAKE PLACID 3** [2010] and **LAKE PLACID: THE FINAL CHAPTER** [2012, all USA]), along with Ian Valentine. The present title was directed by Robert Stadd, and it remains his sole feature film credit under this capacity. He is a very successful visual effects producer and supervisor, who's been working in said field since 1991, and he has worked on such mainstream films as Chuck Russell's **THE MASK** (1994, USA).

The acting department is far more interesting, as other than the two leads mentioned above, you get decent performances from talent such as Lilas Lane (**YESTERDAY WAS A LIE** [2008, USA]), Nathan Anderson (**GODZILLA** [1998, USA/Japan; see *Monster!* #5, p.21]), Michael Cory Davis (**ALIEN APOCALYPSE** [2005, USA; see *M!* #13, p.51]), Ray Baker (**TOTAL RECALL** [1990, USA]), Carl Weathers (**PREDATOR** [USA, 1987]), George Zlatarev (**I SPIT ON YOUR GRAVE 2** [2013, USA]), Vladimir Nikolov (**ALIEN LOCKDOWN** [2004, USA; see *M!* #14, p.54]), Atanas Srebrev (**WICKED LITTLE THINGS** [2006, USA]), Julian Vergov (**THE FOURTH KIND** [2009, USA/UK]), Svezhen Mladenov (**THE LEGEND OF HERCULES** [2014, USA]), Daniel Tzotchev (**SHARK ZONE** [2003, USA/Bulgaria]), Dejan Angelov (**RAPTOR ISLAND** [2004, USA]), Boris Pankin (**REIGN OF THE GARGOYLES** [2007, USA]), Jonas Talkington (**MAN WITH THE SCREAMING BRAIN** [2005, USA/Germany]), Kiril Efremov (**SOFIA** [2012, USA]), Panayot Tzanev (**I AM DAVID** [2003, USA]), and Velizar Binev (**HITMAN** [2007, USA/France]).

Ehh, one last thing I'd like to add is, can anyone explain to me this film's obsession with numbers? There appears to be at all times somebody talking about how many thousands were acquired by the army, how many thousands died, etc. You *won't* be able to keep track!

BREEDERS

Reviewed by Eric Messina

USA, 1986. D: Tim Kincaid

Wizard Video narration: *"Prepare yourself for the arrival of the sexual parasites known as—***BREEDERS***! The invasion has begun, but these aliens* don't want *to phone home, and they don't want to consume human flesh. They don't even want to control the Earth. What these aliens want are*...Earth women! *And not just* any *woman. The invasion has begun: from the* inside *out*... **BREEDERS**! *If you haven't been able to get a date lately, maybe you're lucky."*

MGM VHS blurb: *"They're Gonna Love You...'Til You're Dead!"*

In the mid-'80s, I saw this on the video store horror shelf along with Tobe Hooper's **LIFEFORCE** (1985, UK/USA [see *Monster!* #12, p.9]) and **DEF-CON 4** (1985, Canada, D: Paul Donovan), but would not be able to watch it until years later when I was old enough. I tend to associate the Reagan/Bush era with frightening memories of nuclear disaster and the dreaded red button that could be activated at any moment, decimating the entire global population. There were a lot of Cold War made films at the time, but **BREEDERS** was not one of them, though. I just associate the videotape with this time period, and sadly had to stick to alien flicks that didn't feature luscious bare boobs in them. The big-box Wizard Video cover really grabbed me, though. Young as I was, I didn't even know what rape was at that time, but these half-naked women being dragged forcibly away by a bug-eyed beast manning horny tractor tentacles on the cover looked like they were definitely being intergalactically assaulted in a sexual way. The first time I got to see this dopey alien rape fantasy opus was on Impact, one of the best channels On Demand; they show practically everything that came out from The Cannon Group, the legendary Golan and Globus studio.

If you thought Bill Malone's **SCARED TO DEATH** (1980, USA [which I reviewed in *Monster!* #15, p.43]) was dumb and had lobotomized actors, just wait till you see the brain trusts walking around in *this* heap. When you watch **BREEDERS**, you know what you're getting into, and the movie taps into every trashy nerve you'd expect it to hit…that's how much *fun* it is! I've never seen a Tim Kincaid film that I've enjoyed up until now. (He used to work in gay porn under the pseudonym "Joe Gage".)

Dr. Gamble Pace, played by attractive African-American actress Teresa Farley, shows up first and delivers her lines with a vacant stare, often resembling a deer caught in headlights. The research computer she uses at the lab looks like the same one from Jeff Kanew's **REVENGE OF THE NERDS** (1984, USA) that Gilbert (Anthony Edwards) utilizes to snag a date with Judy (Michelle Meyrink)!

At the Manhattan General Hospital, an alien invader—disguised as a friendly German man out walking his schnauzer, of all things—attacks a virgin. When Donna (played by Natalie O'Connell) arrives at the hospital, it turns out she was just one of many victims recently raped by aliens. The victim is first drugged then attacked by the creatures, which use various human guises to fool their unsuspecting female Earthling prey.

Next we meet a curly-haired, thick-browed bikini model (they play this goofy overly-dramatic synthesizer music throughout that's hysterical to hear!). She does a line of coke just before launching into a nice round of nude gymnastics. This pretty brunette is played by Frances Raines, who's actually related—she's his grandniece—to Claude Rains, famed for his roles as **THE INVISIBLE MAN** (1933, USA, D: James Whale) and as Larry Talbot's father in **THE WOLF MAN** (1941, USA, D: George Waggner). Sadly, in **BREEDERS** Ms. Raines becomes the next victim, as the creature—which looks like a giant green-eyed fly—rips through some random dude named Ted's chest, Ridley Scott's **ALIEN**-style, then has his evil way with her.

The transformation sequences are pretty hammy, which are not the fault of effects genius Ed French (the actors themselves are more to blame). Sometimes they'll just show the monster's slimy paw, which looks like it's covered in tar. The over-amorous creeps like to hang out in the sewers (man, it sure must be *crowded* down there, what with Breeders and C.H.U.D.'s and Syngenors all bumbling around, stepping on each other's toes!).

They make the sewer system look spacious and actually clean, and, even though these elements work in its favor, the production designer did a terrible job.

One male character claims that "No one is beyond suspicion when it comes to rape", this right after he figures out that the alien can assume the identity of anyone, a concept too ambitious for *this* rickety special effects team. It pains me to say this, but coming from the very capable and inventive makeup creature creator Mr. French, the special effects

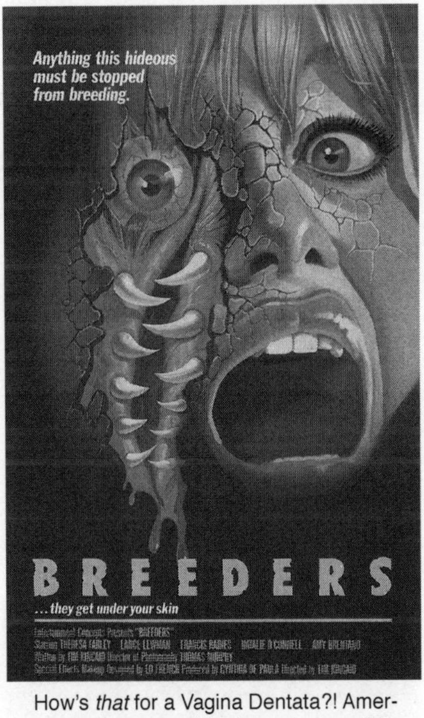

How's *that* for a Vagina Dentata?! American tradepaper ad for the notorious '80s anti-masterpiece (art unsigned). This same eye-catching artwork later found its way onto Turkish posters for Stan Winston's **PUMPKINHEAD** (1988, USA)

are frankly pretty weak. He has worked on everything from Larry Cohen's **THE STUFF** (1985, USA) to Nick Zedd's films, including **GEEK MAGGOT BINGO** (1983, USA). He's one of the best FX artists in monster cinema, and has been involved with Kincaid on many occasions, but for some reason none of his ghastly effects are showcased here.

A cute blonde nurse named Kathleen (Lee Anne Baker) strips in front of the stove. Hey, wait a second. Am I watching **DON'T ANSWER THE PHONE!** (1980, USA, D: Robert Hammer) again? No, because there are tons of gratuitous naked scenes like this, which I'm pretty sure are mainly here to distract you from the shoddy alien effects. I want to pin the blame on Kincaid for deciding to dial back the monster effects, but French has worked with him on numerous occasions, so I have no idea why they come off so cheesy here.

The blonde nurse is an "old-fashioned fuddy-duddy" and wants to save her virginity until marriage; too bad an alien lifeform assaults her. Apologies to Ed French, but it's hard for me to believe he really worked on this film. Sadly, the aliens in **BREEDERS** are just so *awful*, I feel as if they had a rubber monster glove found at the dollar store that they intermittently slipped on to grope at various girls with when needed. If you're looking for attractive ladies being mauled by shadowy beasts, then this one's got you covered. It takes that tentacle-rape fetish started in B.D. Clark's **GALAXY OF TERROR** (1981, USA) and attempts to replicate it,

BREEDERS was so awesome it got a 1996 remake that was even cheaper looking!

with poor results (at least special effects-wise). However, what it lacks in convincing latex effects, it seriously makes up for in campiness and unintentional hilarity.

Don't trust any males in this film, as it seems like they are all potential alien rapists in the middle of an extraterrestrial orgasm, raining sinewy flesh and blood on the walls.

Dale Andriotti (Lance Lewman), the pasty detective who shares an office with the pretty black doctor played by the aforementioned Ms. Farley, does a little investigating on Ted's mom. She mentions that he used to hang out in underground tunnels (which seems like gay sex club "**CRUISING** [1980, USA] hanky-in-the-back-pocket"-type code to me). So, there's no way he would try to assault Frances Raines. You'd think the case would close right then and there, but it gets even wilder!

Donna, the first victim, stabs a hospital orderly, then escapes; in fact, all the girls who did the nasty with the saucer-men go into a trance and venture down into the cesspits.

BREEDERS has the straight juvenile male advantage over most other sewer-dweller monster movies, because it shows tons of female flesh. Had I known there was another movie about creatures living beneath the catacombs in the city's bowels that showed truckloads of naked women, you can bet the then-10-year-old me most likely would have passed over **C.H.U.D.** (1984, USA, D: Douglas Cheek) for this one instead. But this movie doesn't even compare to that masterpiece, so I would've missed-out.

You won't believe how gross the galactic semen bath/hot tub scene is! When they do at long last finally show us an actual monster onscreen, it looks like a cyclops that has a vaginal opening in its face filled with razor teeth. Mr. French shows up in a non-speaking role, and he transforms into the creature seen on the cover. I'm thinking they had only a few dollars to really show off some bursting bladders and latex, because the gruesome level starts rising toward the end. Even though **BREEDERS** is cheesy as hell, it's worth sticking around for the ending. For more on the film, here are some other tidbits related or not (you decide): besides being a derogatory term gay people apply to straights, The Breeders, as most alternative music fans know, were a Pixies spinoff group. The message this film left me with was that you can never trust a male, especially a sex-starved UFO-traveling one.

Make sure to break out a case of beer with the highest legally allowed alcohol content before you view this one!

THE BLACK HOLE

Reviewed by Christos Mouroukis

USA/Germany, 2006. D: Tibor Takács

Ad-line: *"No Force From This World Can Stop It!"*

Harry: "Cookie, do you know what a black hole is?"
Cookie: "Sure, that's how I make my livin'!"
(You see, Cookie is a prostitute, and she is referring to her butt. I couldn't resist quoting this dialogue excerpt from Woody Allen's *Deconstructing Harry* [1997, USA]!)

A bunch of scientists' calculations, when they experiment with radioactivity, go wrong (don't they always?), and things on the one hand go bad for the environment (hence the title) and on the other hand they unleash a maze of electricity that actually takes the form of a creature (think of *The Amazing Spider-Man* comic books' supervillain Electro), and it is on the move from the lab, heading towards the city by travelling through power lines. Panic ensues, and the citizens jump in their cars and evacuate St. Louis, but this could also be because they were thinking of what the electricity bill will look like after all is said and done. (Eh, okay, some times my jokes are worse than others…)

The screenplay by David Goodin (who is usually an assistant accountant on more high-concept films, such as Sam Raimi's **DRAG ME TO HELL** [2009, USA]), which was based on a story by Boaz Davidson and Kenneth Badish (the film's producers) may sound really silly on paper, but the end result is really not that bad. Think of the works of M. Night Shyamalan; certainly not of his **THE SIXTH SENSE** (1999, USA) and **UNBREAKABLE** (2000, USA) era, but more something in the vein of **THE VILLAGE** (2004, USA) and **THE HAPPENING** (2008, USA/France/India).

It is for certain that the film under review with its budget of $3,500,000 (and its reuse of shots from **CATEGORY 6: DAY OF DESTRUCTION** [2004, USA]) cannot compete with the gazillion-dollars crap-fests mentioned above (for one thing, on one of the scientists' computers the very "otherworldly" screensaver of Windows Media Player is shown, which reminded me of how great it seemed to my teenage eyes a couple of decades ago when I wanted to make an entire music video out of it, but that project luckily never materialized). However, thanks to director Tibor Takács' experience and skill it remains a fun ride throughout its entire running time. Takács was born in Hungary and had his first hits in the '80s when he directed the horror fan favorites **THE GATE** (1987) and **THE GATE II: TRESPASSERS** (1990, both Canada/USA). He was directing mainly TV series and TV movies during most of the '90s and '00s. He recently came back theatrically with a vengeance when he helmed the awesome **SPIDERS** (2013, USA), and now has many upcoming projects in various states of production.

Various familiar faces parade across the screen, and these include Kristy Swanson (who played the titular role in **BUFFY THE VAMPIRE SLAYER** [1992, USA]), Judd Nelson (**THE BREAKFAST CLUB** [1985, USA]), David Selby (**THE SOCIAL NETWORK** [2010, USA]), Heather Dawn (**SAW II** [2005, USA/Canada]), Christa Campbell (who of course started as a *Playboy* cover-girl, went on to star in popular genre fare such as **DAY OF THE DEAD** [2008, USA] and is now producing money-making films such as **TEXAS CHAINSAW 3D** [2013, USA]), Peter Mayer (**APPARITIONAL** [2014, USA]), James Anthony (**KILLSHOT** [2008, USA]), Daniel Buran (**HELLRAISER: REVELATIONS** [2011, USA]), Tim Snay (**DARK HOUSE** [2009, USA]), and Ermal Williamson (whom you will see in the upcoming **STAR QUEST** [2015, USA], which is currently in post-production).

'80s Venezuelan VHS box

EVIL IN THE WOODS

Reviewed by Dennis Capicik

USA, 1986. D: William J. Oates

Produced at the height of the VHS boom during the '80s, **EVIL IN THE WOODS** probably had at least some aspirations towards being released theatrically, but it was most likely mainly geared towards the home video market right from its inception. However, in an ironic twist of fate, the final product never even got an official release in the US, unless you consider the rather dubious Puerto Rican VHS (which showed up in numerous North American vid stores) as an "official" release.

Opening with familiar aerial shots of some nondescript forest—made all the more ominous with typical '80s synth laid over the picture—this overly-long credit sequence eventually reveals the city of Atlanta, Georgia as we are quickly introduced to Brian (Brian Abent), a rather precocious kid on his way to the public library. Once there, he almost immediately becomes intrigued by a giant book entitled *Evil in the Woods*, which he borrows without hesitation. Naturally, this book serves as the framing device for our "fractured fable", and, although cheap in execution, everything seems fairly straightforward up to this point...that is, until the film proper begins. For reasons known only to the filmmakers, the action opens in 1956 in Mildew, Georgia, where, we are told, "pure evil has reigned for 3000 years"; this as a driver is run off the road and he screams at some unidentified presence. With the help of an impromptu narrator with a comedic southern drawl (even Brian remarks rather inquisitively, "Who said that?"), the film moves ahead to the present day as a low-budget film crew is shooting "BIGFOOT VS. THE SPACE KILLERS" *[Sounds like ideal* Monster! *fare – ed.]* in those very same (quote) "nasty, nasty" woods. Of course, they soon encounter titular "evil in the woods", which turns out to be an evil old witch named Ida, who, along with her minions, eventually slaughter most of the film crew in the gory finale.

Obviously presented as a comedy, this is an absolute *mess* of a film, which at times even spoofs itself, as when the director of the fictional film comments that he would like to "make some films that matter, with substance and maturity"; even the local sheriff comments on the silliness of one their earlier productions, "BARNYARD ANIMALS OF THE LIVING DEAD" *[Ditto! – ed]*. At one point, as wolves howl in the background, the film crew sits around the fire telling campfire stories about a "strange creature that lives in Florida" with "seven feet of teeth gleaming in the moonlight". Meanwhile, a young couple camping nearby is growing increasingly concerned after they are unable to locate their son, who, unknown to them, has been abducted by Ida, dismembered (off-screen) and cooked in a pot! When they contact the local law officer (appropriately named Sheriff Dolts!), he actually turns out to be in cahoots with Ida, and with the help of some magic potion concocted using the dead boy's flesh, makes herself beautiful once again (i.e., lots of overdone '80s-styled makeup and big, teased-up hair!). Our narrator occasionally interjects to help with the story exposition, and c/o sloppy inter-titles—at one point "shadow" is misspelled "shawdow"—the filmmakers try to make sense of everything. The film crew eventually begins to disappear one-by-one, and when their "star" Dick (Dennis Klein) goes missing after having too much to drink and too much "tootski" (i.e., coke), the double-entendres are let loose as "they all look for *DICK*"; the next day our narrator actually intones, "the story continues even with the absence of *DICK*." At this point, even Brian is becoming restless as he rolls his eyes in frustration, but thankfully, this freaky fairy tale finally picks up the pace for the gory finale when Ida's "children" morph into monsters and she casts a new spell ("Powers of evil...turn this mortal into a creature of the night!") on the rest of the film crew. Of course, like any '80s horror flick, the ending is left open-ended for a possible follow-up "fractured fable", and even Brian succumbs to the book's malevolent power.

Shot on 16mm, this is admittedly pretty awful stuff, with stilted line delivery, unfunny dialogue and poor cutting, but, at the same time, there's enough general weirdness to keep things interesting in that "head-scratching" sort of way. The filmmaker's tongues were, quite obviously, firmly planted in their cheeks when they embarked on this, and it honestly looks as if most of it was made up on the spot; monsters, witches, cannibalism and some enthusiastic gore are all thrown into the plot without any rhyme or reason whatsoever. Even at the standard 90-minute running time, it's far too long, but, despite the amateurism and a story that doesn't make a lick of sense, this is still mindlessly entertaining. However, for the uninitiated, be forewarned: approaching this expecting any semblance of something coherent will surely end in disappointment—or perhaps even outright resentment—for subjecting yourself to such truly unruly and slovenly filmmaking.

Not much is known about director William J. Oates, but the film's distributor Cinevest (now called Cinevest Interactive) is owned and operated by Arthur Schweitzer, who also distributed many other no-budget flicks like Mark Nowicki's **THE NOSTRIL PICKER** (1987) and Brett Piper's **MUTANT WAR** (1988, both USA). Like many of these lowly Schweitzer-distributed titles, **EVIL IN THE WOODS** also went MIA in the US, and only ever appeared on Australian, Japanese and Puerto Rican videocassette. As awful as it is, it's quite strange that this never received a domestic VHS release back in the '80s, considering the glut of crap that took up space in video stores back then; just think of Don Swan's **GORE-MET, ZOMBIE CHEF FROM HELL** (1986) or B. Dennis Wood's **DEATH ROW DINER** (1988, both USA) for unwatchable, bottom-of-the-barrel flicks which were readily available on many North American video store shelves during the same timeframe.

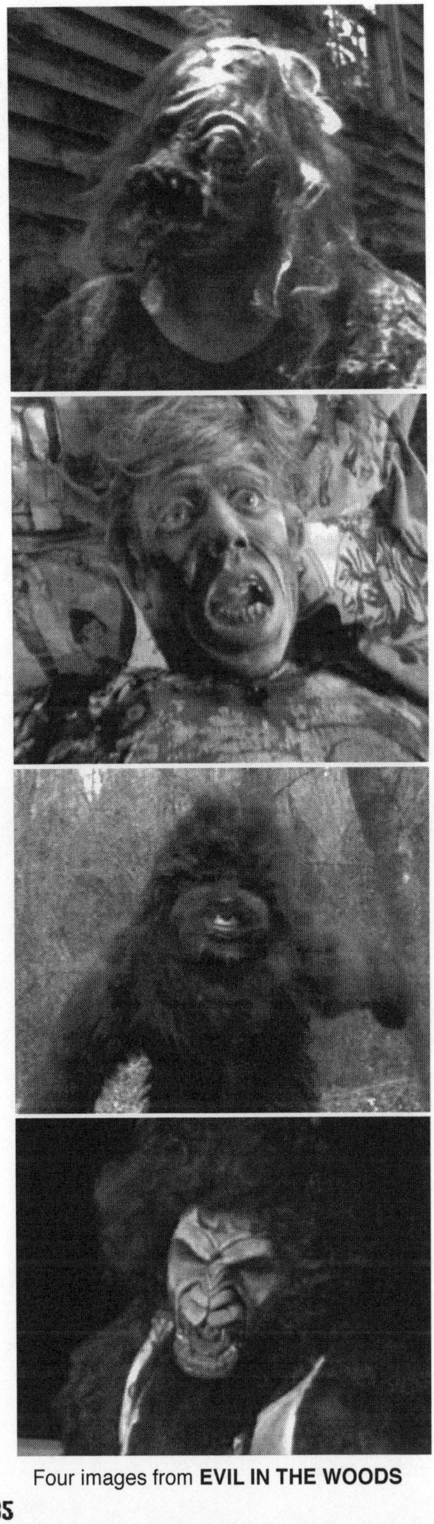

Four images from **EVIL IN THE WOODS**

THE SLIME PEOPLE

Reviewed by Mark Savage

USA, 1963. D: Robert Hutton

Our childhood memories tend to focus on one aspect of the films that shaped our imaginations and made us the obsessives we are today. For me, **THE VALLEY OF GWANGI** (1969, USA) was all about cowboys fighting dinosaurs, and I didn't

Judee Morton gets slimed in this US lobbycard

recall anything else about the film when I saw it again through adult eyes. **IT'S ALIVE!** (1969, USA), the Larry Buchanan horror—a flick that once baked my preteen brain—was about a thing (I've always loved "things", because I sympathize with them) living in a cave in the woods, and that alone gave me a claustrophobic recall of the film. **THE SLIME PEOPLE**? Well, that was about creatures jumping out at you from thick, soupy fog, and they brandished spears, and their murders were accompanied by a soundtrack that was a cacophony of bubbles and odd sounds akin to muffled farts. But it was the *fog* that I remembered most, because those things were in that fog, and you couldn't stop that fog from catching up with you. The fog just made a guy real anxious, especially when he was six.

When I saw Robert Hutton's **THE SLIME PEOPLE** again when I was all grown up, it was like watching an extended cut of the film, because there were bits and pieces in it that had nothing to do with slime people, spears, and fog: women, for example—there were two of them—and there was a lot of driving around, too, on the same roads, and the director seemed very interested in staging a bunch of fluff at "Curly's Meat Market", where three pounds of bacon could be had for a buck, and steaks went out the door for eighty-nine cents. My preteen head didn't hold onto these details because they weren't monster-related, and I didn't recall the ladies at all because I wasn't thinking about the opposite sex at six years old seated in my parents' lounge room at 1 a.m. wrapped in a blanket large enough to be a circus tent. No doubt about it, those were the days! Those were breathless days when monsters held you in their grip. And still do.

THE SLIME PEOPLE was in constant rotation in the late '60s and '70s on Melbourne's Channel 0 (now Channel 10). Deadly Earnest, the resident horror host *[see sidebar, p.40]*, would rise from his coffin—which was also fog-filled—address viewers, wish them a "ghastly evening", converse with "Claw", his deformed hand, then introduce the movie. Every now and then, during ad-breaks, he'd read viewer mail, make nasty faces, and cackle. The fanged, top-hatted Deadly wasn't a pleasant fellow to look at. His flesh was ruddy, his eye fucked, and his teeth were more like a collection of broken piano keys. He had a mean spirit, too, and waged war with a mail-eating thing called Igor. Igor would eat Deadly's fan mail after Deadly had read it out loud under a spooky light, and deliver an almighty burp. To the six-year-old me, Deadly was subversive…and that's why I loved him.

His movies were mostly Z-grade, with no discernible stars or story logic. **THE BLOB** (1958, USA), which had a star, was an exception, but that didn't

US one-sheet poster

play as often as **THE SLIME PEOPLE, IT! THE TERROR FROM BEYOND SPACE** (1958, USA), **IT'S ALIVE!**, or **THE BEAST WITH A MILLION EYES** (1955, USA). I loved all of them, but I definitely felt ripped-off by the Beast when I failed to count more more than five or six eyes. What the hell had happened to those extra eyes?! Was Santa Claus a lie, too?

THE SLIME PEOPLE delivers now, delivered then, and will keep on delivering if you can ignore the crummy acting and miserable writing.

The film wastes no time at all foregrounding its monsters. In an advanced peek at the slimy goodness to come, the opening shot features a Slime Man emerging from a metal grate; following that iconic image is a speared corpse washed up on the beach. The camera then pans off the corpse to the empty beach so "The Slime People" can ripple into view. We're then introduced to a bloke trying to land an airplane (Tom Gregory), who's warned by a voice in Santa Barbara to stay out of LA. Not heeding the warning, he lands, anyway, although the airport he lands in doesn't look one bit like LA—and it's not as foggy as we're told it is on the radio, either—and finds himself alone.

Tom, who's a sportscaster for KTTV, attempts to make a call. Phone's dead, of course, but, never mind, a car with a university professor named Galbraith and his two hot daughters, Lisa and Bonnie, rolls up. Tom jumps in and, before you can say, "Cue exposition!" pretty Bonnie, the younger daughter, launches into an explanation of what the hell is happening: "First the Slime People came, the Army came to fight them and lost, and they built a big wall after everyone evacuated."

Naturally, Tom thinks the Prof and his hot daughters are wacky until he comes face-to-face with the "Slime Men" (Bonnie's description) himself. With this exposition out of the way, Hutton gets to focus on a mess of confined action scenes while adding a younger hero, Cal, to the mix. Within three minutes, Cal lays hands on Bonnie—who doesn't mind—and tells her he's "not the kind of guy who kisses *any* girl". No, pal, you only kiss girls when you're stuck in a meat locker with them, and Slime Men with whiskers are battering on the doors with spears! But it isn't only Cal who gets the girl. Tom, the sportscaster, quickly puts the moves on the slightly older Lisa as the good old Prof pretends not to notice his daughters being systematically lined-up to be laid.

Once the romantic filler is put to bed, so to speak, the focus returns to the monsters, and we get an eyeful of half-a-dozen of them, each kind of unique and ugly in their own individual way. A major feature of these creatures is their curved, protruding spine. Their faces tend to vary, but their build, their posture, their stooped appearance, is consistent. Looking at them now, I can't help thinking that they resemble *Doctor Who*'s Zygons mixed with the reptilian Silurians. *Who*, of course, first aired the same year **THE SLIME PEOPLE** was made,

SLIME PEOPLE model by Mark Glassy

A Zygon from vintage *Doctor Who*

so perhaps someone at the BBC caught the flick and liked the monsters enough to later replicate aspects of them. The present film's creatures do have subterranean origins, as did the Silurians and Sea Devils, and they were only forced to the surface because their home beneath the earth had been disturbed by atomic testing, so goes the Prof's spot-on speculation.

The swirling fog in **THE SLIME PEOPLE** is not only there to hide the nonexistent production values: it *does* have a purpose. The Slime Men are creating fog in order to lower the outside temperature; they would then be able to live comfortably above ground. The mission of our heroes, then, is to somehow disable the fog-making machine that has created a nasty wall and, hopefully, wipe out the slimers with it. The science is a little flimsy on this matter, but it follows that the slimers' machine not only creates fog, but the fog forms a solid dome over Los Angeles, and nobody can enter or exit this dome. Shades of Stephen King here... or, more correctly, King's *Under The Dome* (2009) possesses shades of **THE SLIME PEOPLE**. Chances are he saw it, and the central conceit buried itself in his psyche. In any event, it's a clever idea that contains our heroes, and allows the production to smother itself in fog—not that the fog is entirely convincing, of course. Much of the time, it is optical (added later), so it moves when the camera moves, and is often just a dark murk obscuring the action.

The action on tap here is of the Monster Versus Human variety, and the fighting resembles World Championship Wrestling more than the brutal, bloody combat of contemporary monster flicks. The Slime Men are flipped, thrown, and kicked, and spears are driven into their torsos without too much trouble. How these devils defeated the Army is a secret they took to the grave; we certainly don't see any demonstration of amazing fighting abilities here—perhaps they were all a bit pooped by the time our heroes stumbled onto their foggy conspiracy?

As monster pics go, this beauty keeps the monsters coming, and the simple logic of the piece holds the film together. Director Hutton is also the film's star, and he acquits himself only adequately. William Boyce, as the horny military kid, has trouble walking straight, let alone delivering a believable line. The two ladies, Susan Hart and Judee Morton, exude an enthusiasm about being in a real movie that isn't quite consistent with the peril their characters find themselves in; Hart later played **THE GHOST IN THE INVISIBLE BIKINI** (1966, USA). Robert Burton doesn't have a lot to do as Professor Galbraith except watch his daughters get fondled and occasionally speculate about the origins or grand plans of the title's

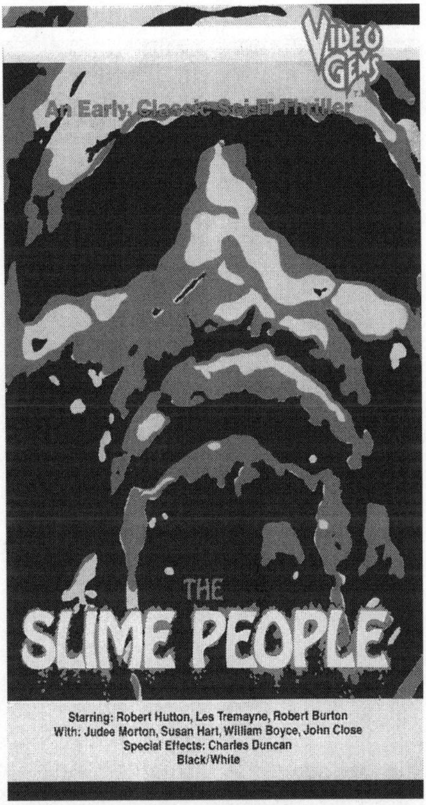

'80s US VHS box

subterranean namesakes. Les Tremayne, however, does a fun turn as a character named Norman Tolliver. When our heroes come across him, Hutton as Tom Gregory describes him thus: "...he's a great writer, but he's the greatest troublemaker I've ever known." As absolutes go, Tom's comment is quite a doozy. Tolliver, of course, doesn't believe in Slime People, so he's rather surprised when he ends up as one of the creatures' lunch.

Described as "self-sealing" by Professor Galbraith, the Slime People are finally defeated by an arrow aimed at their fog machine, which resembles an old, puffed-up vacuum cleaner bag. Once deflated, the slimers lose steam and perish. But the Prof, though relieved, does speculate that "perhaps even stranger creatures live underground", and on that point he's 100% accurate.

The black-and-white glory of **THE SLIME PEOPLE** endures, and each time I return to it, I contemplate again that when we love films, we return to the same films over and over again, because films are captured memories, the feelings they give rise to cleverly coded into their flickering images.

DEADLY EARNEST FROM DOWN UNDER

Hedley Cullen as Adelaide's Deadly Earnest, with his pet skull Yorick

Ian Bannerman as Sydney's Deadly Earnest

During the 1960s and '70s, a number of different performers—some four in all—played the character Deadly Earnest on television stations in various regions of Australia.

Comedian and ex-propman Ralph Baker—the version Australian-born, American-based Mark Savage grew up with—played him Friday nights on ATV-0 in Melbourne from 1967-72. Mark remembers: "His show was *Aweful Movies with Deadly Earnest*. I once met him, because he appeared at our primary school's annual fete. I was the only one not scared of him. I just worshipped him, and my parents were concerned. Even my mum said he was 'awful'. (*Haha!*) He was very nasty. Not even trying to be funny. Just a rotten guy; unrepentant prick. That's why I liked him! I'm sure it was meant to be an act, but Baker seemed to enjoy being sadistic and belligerent. He was the first person on TV (to me) who didn't put on an act. No airs. Even at 6 or 7, I perceived the difference. I thank him for that... It's like the job gave him the opportunity to be truly 'awful' and pretend it was a joke."

Ralph Baker as Melbourne's Deadly Earnest

Films screened by the various Earnests over the years included this ish's **THE SLIME PEOPLE**, **ROBOT MONSTER** (1953, USA), **CARNIVAL OF SOULS** (1962, USA), **REPTILICUS** (1961, USA/Denmark), and **THE GIANT GILA MONSTER** ([1959, USA] reviewed by Mark's Aussie countryman John Harrison in *Monster!* #13, p.62). In Adelaide, Hedley Cullen played the character of Deadly Earnest from 1967 on into the '70s. From 1966-68 on Sydney's TEN Channel 10, he was played by English-born Ian Bannerman. During the early '70s, Shane Porteous played him in Brisbane. Each "version" of the character had their own distinctly different look. During the late '60s, Earnest even featured for a time on Sydney radio.

Bill Webb wrote an article entitled "Deadly Earnest from Down Under" in *Scary Monsters* magazine (#7, June 1993). Deadly Earnest is not to be confused with several American horror show hosts named Dead Earnest, who were active within roughly the same general timeframe. ~ **Les Moore**

For more info, visit:

http://myweb.wvnet.edu/e-gor/tvhorrorhosts/hostsd.html

http://retrorocket.tripod.com/Deadly/DE-MEL1.html

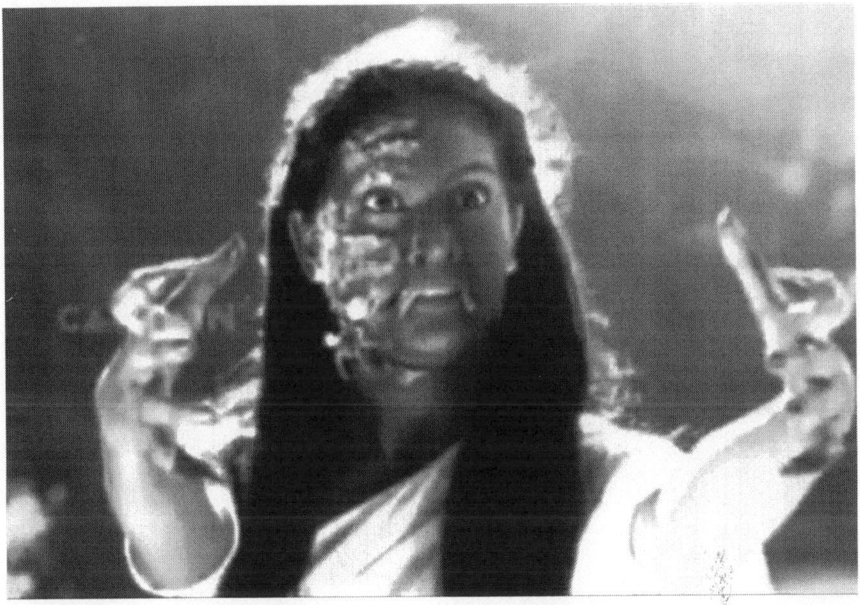

PYASI APSARA

Reviewed by Tim Paxton

India, 1991. D: K.S. Gopalakrishnan

PYASI APSARA / प्यासी अप्सरा (Hindi title) roughly translates as "Thirsty Nymph", and what transpires in the film pretty much substantiates this title. The movie is all about a lustful "nymph" who is out to kill as many men as possible. The film is from 1991, a time when the Ramsay family, with their traditionally trashy brand of frightful filmmaking, began their quick demise, and director Ram Gopalvarma's **RAAT** was just about to shake up the horror genre. When I first saw the artwork for **PYASI APSARA**'s VCD release (on *induna.com*'s website), I had considered it yet another bit of trashy horror made by the likes of Kanti Shah and his contemporaries. The cover art was very typical of the genre. This artwork features a buxom actress and the all-to-familiar bloody skeletal face (art which was plagiarized from the **CREEPSHOW 2** poster, with fangs added; this image has been integrated into the sleeve designs of many low-budget VCD and DVDs). Little did I know that the film would turn out to be a very cool no-budget monster movie.

The word *pyasi* (or *pyaasi* in some spellings) is a rather common title in the field of thriller and horror films, especially for those whose plotlines involve sexy ladies. Its connotation of "hungry" or "thirsty" add fuel to the exploitation thrill. Other films that use this trigger word include **KHOON KI PYAASI** ("*Thirsty Fear*", 1996, D: K. Chandra), **PYASI CHUDAIL** ("*Hungry Witch*", 1998, D: Rafi), **PYAASI** ("*The Thirst*", 2003, D: Kanti Shah), **PYASI BHOOTNI** ("*The Thirsty Female Ghost*", 2003, D: Kanti Shah), and **PYASI NAGIN** ("*Thirsty Cobra Woman*", 2004, D: Krishan Shah). You get the idea. *Apsara* on the other hand is usually a word used when writing or talking about the classical water/air elemental nymph from Hindu mythology. Traditionally, these female demigods are depicted as very voluptuous creatures which are comparable to the angels of Western/Christian religious beliefs. So, by pairing *pyasi* with *apsara*, you get a very tempting film title indeed. I was surprised that the film actually delivered on this promise with the actress who plays the monster in the film (someone who looks familiar to me but I still can't quite place a name to her face). The names in the credits are your usual mononymous stars who, while quite possibly popular when the film was made, have very little online data as to their filmographies. All the men in the credits I could track down without any problems (Ramu, Jagathi, Vincent, etc.), but who was the actress who played "Betty" in the film? Kapil? Whomever she was, she fits the bill…*big time!*

As the film opens, we find ourselves in some (from the looks of it) southern region of rural/tribal India—possibly Tamil Nadu or Kerala—where we are introduced to all the elements that will set the film in motion. In fact, these are popular motifs that appear in much of the *Junglee* subgenre of adventure film, and it progresses along a predictable path.

Artwork for the VCD release of **PYASI APSARA**, wherein sex & horror comingle successfully

But what distinguishes **PYASI APSARA** from the usual trash is its unusual plot twists. It's a pity that there seemed to be so little in the way of finances to pull this production off properly, but I am very forgiving when it comes to cheap Indian productions. First up is the village doctor (late Malayalam actor Vincent, whose roles typically include police inspectors and priests, as well as physicians), a scholarly medical man who dispenses cures to the needy local tribes people. Men and women come in with various ills and he prescribes pills, ointments, and advice, all the while assisted by a very whiny and annoying office servant (the film's horrid comic relief, a skinny grotesque with a swollen belly, crossed eyes, and a high-pitched "funny" voice. Ugh! I *hate* characters like this!). We also see the doc treat a young man brought in with a cobra bite, for which the wound is sliced and the infected blood then sucked out and spat into a cup. He is a learned and man who is in the community to serve... and also to—surprise, surprise!—conduct secret experiments; but more about that later.

Next up is Betty[1], the doctor's daughter, who is something of a pariah due to her pimply face; but other than for her lumpy facial pockmarks, she is a very attractive young woman. Betty has amorous designs on a handsome local man after he mistakes her for his girlfriend and grabs her from behind, and she thereafter becomes infatuated with him. He, on the other hand, is repulsed by her skin condition, but is nice enough to continue chatting with her about the weather, etc. This one-sided bond is essentially what drives the film...although not in a pleasant direction.

Besides the people of a local village (which I assume are around, but nothing is seen of them, as characters just walk in and out of scenes without much information—pretty much Indian cinema right there!) there is a population of tribals[2] who march through the jungle chanting, wear feathers and beads, brandish spears, and engage in other romantically-inclined action. The film could have been made without these random elements, but my guess is that these tribals are included to add a bit of "local color" and rustic sexiness to this *Junglee* film. In an extended sequence we have a handsome tribesman who is caught making out with his girlfriend by another tribesman. A test of fighting skill follows to see who will claim the woman as his, and the two warriors square-off with spears. When the ritualized skirmish is over and our handsome tribesman—just as expected—wins, that's our cue for a big dance number.[3]

Meanwhile, our doctor/scientist sadly watches Betty his *unmarried* daughter while she sleeps, and in anguish wishes that she wasn't disfigured by her facial blemishes. Distraught, he begins a series of experiments on animals to cure the "ugliness" of her skin. He infuses his scientific knowledge with local herbs and research into his collection of old and ancient books on Vedic knowledge. His daughter secretly witnesses the results of his most recent achievement when her father injects a black rabbit with a serum he has concocted. The dark-hued bunny's fur turns white, and everyone (his daughter included) believes that there is still hope for a cure for her ugliness. If so, maybe Betty will be able to win the heart of her beloved. But, as fate would have it, the good doctor has a heart attack and dies. The villagers cremate his body, while his ungainly assistant attempts to rape Betty, believing that he is the only man worthy of her. Betty is able to fend him off by threatening to cut his balls off with a knife, and she sends for

1 From what I have gleaned via repeat viewings, this seems to be her Western nickname in the film. As the VCD/DVD lacks any subtitles whatsoever, and this is a Hindi dub of what I suspect to originally be a Tamil film, I'll just have to go with "Betty" for this review, I'm afraid.

2 Most countries have groups of people who are stereotyped in their film productions and other media, and for India it is usually the tribal members of their population. India has over 600 distinct tribes; the largest—and most often made-fun-of in films—are the Nagas. They are typically portrayed as buffoons, lustful savages, or else as sweet but backward people. The tribe in **PYASI APSARA** could represent any of the 36 different peoples that inhabit the state of Tamil Nadu, but it is hard to say precisely which one.

3 Contrary to popular belief, incidental songs and dance numbers are not *always* included in Indian films, but they typically do help ticket sales. The fun little numbers that pop up in **PYASI APSARA** are penned by the popular Malayalam film industry composer S. P. Venkatesh.

her "love". He rejects her advances and she falls into a funk when witnessing him making whoopee with another woman. In a fit of desperation, she remembers the magic potion that her late father had concocted, and rummages through his lab's cabinet of chemicals and grabs a vial. She gulps down the liquid, and it immediately takes an effect.

And here is where the film goes off the deep end and gets good! I mean *crazy* good, despite the lack of a budget to speak of, as modern science bumps uglies with the supernatural, and the result is something very Southern. I do so love my Indian horror films with Tamil and Malayalam spice! There is a wonderful earthiness, charm, and (magical) realism to the products of their film industry as a whole, and not just their horror and devotional genres, either. Much of their fantastic films—those which I have seen—prior to the turn of the century have been among my Indian favorites. For anyone interested, check out my piece on Malayalam-language subcontinental horror films in *Weng's Chop* #4.5 (p.108), as I cover numerous titles.

Meanwhile, back in the lab: Betty's booty begins to burn (whether only symbolically or in actuality, I am unsure, as the director of SFX—something to this day that is not often pulled off very well—simply superimposes s faint flame over her image). And not only that, but her skin swells up, her face blisters and oozes pus (in a brief time-lapse effects sequence via the magic of makeup effects by M.O. Devassya, with trick photography by K.S. Mani). She trashes the lab as she thrashes about in agony. Obviously she got ahold of the wrong potion, and she is now rapidly rotting! In a blind panic she dashes from the lab and jumps into a nearby river, where she boils away to a bloody skeleton before slipping beneath the waters.

Later that day, a strange glow appears in the water where she died. The water bubbles and Betty reemerges from the river as a super-buxom goddess dressed in a traditional *nagina* (cobra lady) outfit, symbolizing that she is now the titular *pysai apsara.* Betty's facial deformities have since vanished along with her frumpiness, for she is now a super-hottie, and performs a bodacious dance number to show off her bomb bod. But she is no mere reincarnated water sprite. Oh no: she has returned from the grave on—what else?!—a mission of vengeance! Betty refocuses the lusty desires of her former self into hateful energy by luring and then killing (by ripping out his throat) the man who had previously spurned her. However, that single act of revenge doesn't satiate her, because she is a very thirsty nymph and there are many more men yet to be devoured…

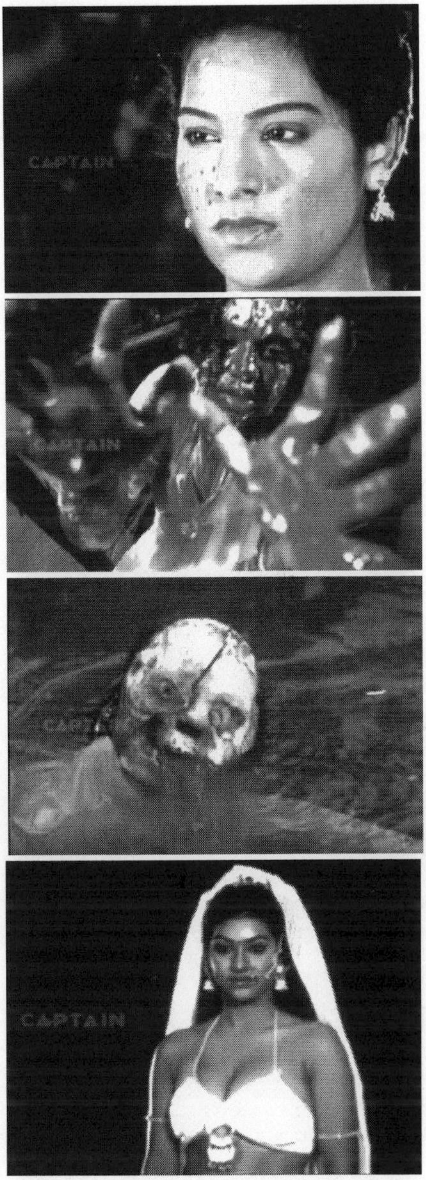

Top to Bottom: The pimply-faced scowl of a young woman scorned who drinks an untested potion to cure her facial affliction. Once drunk, the elixir causes her skin to bubble and boil, and she is reduced to a mess of bloody bones, only to thereafter be reincarnated as a diabolical and very bombastic nymph! Crazy images from **PYASI APSARA**, a Tamil/Malayalam/Hindi fantasy horror film with devotional overtones. The religious imagery—including the spiritual redemption of even the most monstrous of creatures—was not uncommon in films of this kind

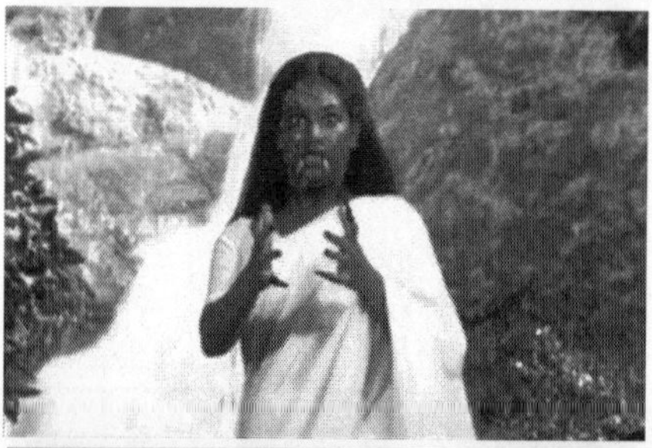

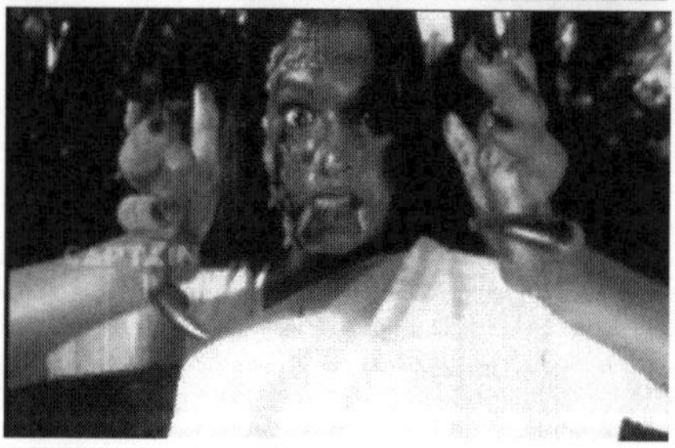

(Meanwhile, we get still more dancing and fighting with the local tribes; but all that pretty much takes a backseat for me in this film. So too do the "comedy" routines that occur when a rich city man arrives in the jungle on a safari with his idiotic hired help in tow. Betty does find and kill a man from the tribe who raped and murdered the girlfriend of his rival. She also devours one of the newcomers, who mistakes her for a local prostitute.)

A holy man (late actor Ravi Menon) wanders into the vicinity, drawn to the village either by chance or possibly due to the karmic nature of recent events. He is a handsome *tantrik*, and Betty fully intends devouring him as well. If only she can seduce him! When he visits a local temple she meets him there and strikes some seductive poses in hopes of getting him horny. The pious priest ignores her and continues on his way. Not to be brushed off so easily, she attempts to entice him yet again with a song and dance number that best shows off her attributes. She changes outfits a few times during the musical number, shakes and shimmies her boobs in front of him. Nada a notice! Then she clones herself (as magical beings are apt to do) so that the two of her can cuddle and nuzzle in front of the holy man to see if *that* will get a rise out of him. He hastens on his way, and Betty stalks him further. When she is repelled by a holy flame that leaps from the man's body, she decides on going somewhere else and kills another man worthy of her sexiness.

The final murder is just too much for our holy hero, and he sets up a *yajna* fire pit to get more information about the rogue *pyasi apsara* and her whereabouts. It seems that the potion which Betty's father prepared and she drank was not intended for her use. Quite possibly her lustful desires and self-centered want to be pretty perverted the positive attributes of the potion and turned consequently her into the bloodthirsty nymph? Whatever's the case, she has to be stopped.

Our priest meets up with Betty once again in the jungle, and this time she doesn't even try to seduce the holy man. She knows the jig is up, but ignores the *tantrik*'s plea to stop her murderous evil ways and be prepared to accept his judgement of reincarnation through holy fire. The *pyasi apsara* ceases to be her gorgeous self and transfoms into a hideous fanged monster, albeit still buxom and bodacious. There is an extended battle of wills and magic as the monster and priest try to outdo each other with phantastic spells. First the female demon grows to gigantic proportions and threatens the man, then he does the same to try and subdue her. When that game of tag doesn't work, she then morphs into a skull-faced horror and attacks him, but is repelled (an effect achieved by having some weird miniature doll shoved into the camera. The simple forced-perspective effects in these sequences, as well as the makeup and Betty's sometimes woman-in-white *chudail* form reminds me of Vinod Talwar's masterpiece **HATYARIN** and its wild effects-filled climax [coincidentally enough, that film was also a 1991 release]). After a few more useless attacks, she transforms into a beastly demon (the traditional wooly-headed, dark-faced and big-teethed South Asian variety) then tosses boulders at the man. The priest decides he's had enough of peaceful confrontation and tosses his walking staff at the monster. The rod sails through the air and transforms into Shiva's *trishula* (trident), striking the troublesome terror and transfixing her against a tree trunk. Thus impaled by the *trishula,* Betty transforms back to her former self: albeit the pus-dribbling, rotting corpse-like version rather than her more appealing visage. She pleads for release, and the holy man listens to her story. He then pulls his staff free of the writhing *apsara*, says a silent prayer, and tosses *holi* powder on Betty. Having received *samsara* (forgiveness), Betty then ascends into the afterlife to await her karmic fate. The End.

PYASI APSARA is a perfect example of the kind of low-budget South Asian filmmaking which I love to discover and savor. The story is rural and very south Indian, originating from the state of Tamil Nadu, I suspect (although the version I screened was dubbed into Hindi. The film was processed and filmed around Madras, which is another name for Chennai, the capital of Tamil Nadu, and its cast and crew is packed with Tamil and Malayalam names). There's not a hint of European influences other than possibly the bit about Betty drinking the scientist's forbidden potion. And that instance is just to get the ball rolling. It isn't until after her rather gruesome death in the lake that a demon takes possession of her body or she is reincarnated as an *apsara* (subtitles would have helped immensely at this point). That addition of the "magical elixir" is irrelevant, as **PYASI APSARA** is really a cautionary tale of lust, murder, vengeance, and ultimately spiritual redemption, all neatly packaged into this little shocker. Of course, the film benefits from the appearance of bombshell wannabe Kapil—*if* that *is* her in the role of Betty, which I've yet to determine with any certainty.

Director K.S. Gopalakrishnan was very active in the Hindi, Malayalam and Tamil industries, beginning in the late 1940s on throughout the 1970s, when he had a string of regional hits. While data on his Tamil- and Malayalam-language films is sketchy at best, his specialty seemed to be devotional films, beginning with **CHAKRADHARI** (which was a surprise hit 1948) or family comedy dramas. He even made delightful mythologicals like **JAI JAGAT JANANI** (1976), **DAIVIYIN THIRUVILAYADAL** (1982), and **MAHASHAKTI MARIAMMAN** (1986), which were lavish productions full of gods and goddesses. By the time the '90s rolled around, Gopalakrishnan had minor box office hits with the actioner **ATHAIMADI METHAIYADI** (1989), the yappy Goddess-based devotional fantasy-drama **MAHA SHAKTI MAA** (1990), and the earthy socio-drama **RANGEEN JAWANI** (1991). Then, out of left field, he made **PYASI APSARA**, which was his first and only horror film that I know of. I do think it's funny that I had to dig around to find anything on this film. It is not listed in Gopalakrishnan's scant filmography on *Wikipedia.com*, nor listed directly on *IMDb.com* as directed by him. I eventually found and verified the date of this film to be 1991 (the DVD had the

When Worlds Collide: *[pp.44-45 pics, from top to bottom]* On the prowl for mortal men to devour, the busty demoness from **PYASI APSARA** attempts to seduce a Hindu holy man. When that doesn't work, it's time to get down to the business of killing him, and she transforms into a toothy *chudail* ("witch"). First she tries a frontal attack with claws; when that tactic fails, she turns into a giantess and tries to squash him! She then transforms into a grotesque devil for the final assault, only to be shish-kabobbed with a holy trident by the priest she so badly wanted to snack on

For those of you who wish to start yourselves a collection of Indian cinema, you may first want to purchase DVDs which actually have English subtitles. Not too many have them, however, if you want to really bulk-up your collection, try buying some of the "3in1" DVD sets which typically run around $1.50 to $3 each. The catch is that these single multi-movie DVDs never have English subtitle options or any bonus material

film's Certificate available—**PYASI APSARA** got an "A" censorship rating, which means this is a film for adults only). Previous Gopalakrishnan productions were fairly well made with decent budgets and big names, and the lackluster production values of **PYASI APSARA** may may reflect one of three things: 1) the film was one of his last directorial efforts, as revenues began to dry up and he turned to more exploitation material (such as his sexploitation vehicle **PAAP PAIT KA**, also from 1991); or 2) the entire film was intentionally meagerly made due to the rather rural setting (there are no sets to speak of, as the majority of the action takes place in and around a jungle setting); or 3) this may have been a personal film for the director and no one wanted to finance the production, since it was in the horror genre (a stigma that would follow such films even until relatively recently, as there is now a glut of ghost films made every year—thank you **THE RING** [1998, Japan] **BLAIR WITCH PROJECT** [1999, USA], and **PARANORMAL ACTIVITY** [2009, USA]!).

Low budget filmmaker J. Neelam made a film of roughly the same name but with the slightly different spelling **PYAASI APSARA**, released in 2004. Neelam is known for his sleazy slapdash spook epics, like **KUWARI CHUDAIL** ("*The Virgin Witch*", 2004) and **MAUT KI DAHSHAT** ("*Horror of Death*", 2004), he did manage to make one of the few Indian comedies I like called **DUPLICATE JAANI DUSHMAN** (2003), which is a spoof that stars Sapna as a rough-and-tumble female bandit who faces down a hairy monster *à la* Rajkumar Kohli's 1979 horror film **JAANI DUSHMAN** ("*The Wife Killer*"). I haven't tracked down that film yet (its VCD is long out-of-print), but the cover makes it appear to be your usual story of an evil *tantrik* run amok. But then again, I had no idea how interesting the Gopalakrishnan film would turn out just by admiring the rather bland cover of the VCD, either.

I have a habit of buying VCDs for their cover art and DVDs for better image quality. In the case of **PYASI APSARA**, it was included in one of those cheap $2.99 "3in1"package deals. It is by far the best film on this DVD; the other two being Indian remakes of Western horror films. Gopalakrishnan's film is at least 100% Indian in its own unique way, as **LADIES HOSTEL** is Ramesh Kumar's horror film with a purloined plot from Lucio Fulci's 1987 **AENIGMA**, and **LADY KILLER** is Chandra Mohan's equally blatant rip-off of Willian Friedkin's 1990 supernatural thriller **THE GUARDIAN**. All three, by the way, are South Indian films and very watchable even without English subtitles.

SHE DEVIL

Reviewed by Dennis Capicik

USA, 1957. D: Kurt Neumann

Text and narration from 20th Century Fox/Regal Films' US trailer: *"A Young Scientist Discovers A Cure-All Serum... And Performs The Most Fantastic Experiment... Ever Conceived By The Human Mind! ...Only six hours, and a beautiful girl on the precipice of death, brought back to normal health, suddenly, miraculously... A woman sound of body, but with a warped, ruthless soul, who will stop at nothing to satisfy her bold desires! ... Every Moment Gripping With Excitement And Suspense! As Nothing Can Stop The Evil Injected Into A Woman's Heart!"*

Although masquerading as a "horror" quickie, Kurt "**KRONOS**" Neumann's sparse-yet-handsomely-lensed **SHE DEVIL** is more akin to a film noir, but the mere fact that a pair of eager, well-to-do scientific types jointly "create" our titular monster—the so-called "She Devil"—certainly warrants its inclusion in these monstercentric pages.

Dr. Dan Scott (Jack Kelly) is an esteemed biochemist who develops a serum based on the fruit fly and its "process of adaptation" in the hopes that mankind will develop a tolerance and adaptability to certain diseases and injuries. Despite being revered by the hospital's administrator, Dr. Richard Bach (Albert Dekker of **DR. CYCLOPS** fame), who also happens to sponsor his research and gives him free room and board at his spacious house, he is naturally skeptical about some of Dr. Scott's results. After a tawny-colored leopard with life-threatening wounds is miraculously cured-with Dr. Scott's drug, it also becomes "unusually vicious", as well as turning *black* in the process. Even though it has some glaring—and unexplainable—side-effects, Dr. Scott proceeds to test his drug on Kyra Zelas (Mari Blanchard), who is suffering from terminal tuberculosis. As expected, the drug works brilliantly, but, much like Dr. Scott's leopard, Kyra soon develops a vicious streak in her behavior, which eventually leads to murder.

Far-fetched and quite silly in concept, **SHE DEVIL** (based on a 1935 short story by "John Jessel"/ Stanley G. Weinbaum *[see p.50]*) is nonetheless highly entertaining, even if many times for the wrong reasons. Mari Blanchard is perfectly cast as the deceptive yet equally alluring siren Kyra, who realizes her power early on and takes full advantage of it. Released into the care of both Dr. Scott and Dr. Bach, Kyra decides to go shopping, and, in a sudden and unexpected move (!), she clobbers a customer over the head with a marble ashtray and steals his money. Panic-stricken, she runs into the change-room, where, in fit of "emotional disturbance", her hair turns blonde, and nobody, including the investigating police officers, even figures it out. Dr. Bach senses trouble right from the outset, but Dr. Scott is "behaving like a lovesick boy" too much to notice the sudden change for the worse in Kyra, and merely comments on her newly-acquired lingerie ("*Ooh la la!*"). Even when the scientists both come to the realization that they've created a monster, Kyra simply replies, "You created me and I'm your responsibility"; and she believes this gives her the freedom to do just as she pleases, which she does without any qualms whatsoever, especially when she realizes she is also—*bonus!*—virtually indestructible because of the ongoing healing powers, or so-called "adaptive ability", of the drug. At a ritzy dinner party held at Dr. Bach's estate, she meets Barton Kendall (John Archer) and his wife Evelyn (Fay Baker), a rich industrialist who immediately falls for her as she seductively enters the party all done-up in a slinky black dress, ready to pounce (pun intended) on anyone she can sink her claws into. That night, she changes her

US half-sheet poster

She-devil Kyra Zelas, as described in "John Jessel"/Stanley G. Weinbaum's original story: *"The girl moved lithe as a panther... Silver-eyed, aluminum-haired, alabaster pale... beyond doubt the most beautiful woman he had ever seen!"*

hair color back to black and dons a matching cape, and, like a cypher of death—almost predating Barbara Steele's look from Bava's **BLACK SUNDAY** (*La maschera del demonio*, 1960, Italy)—kills Kendall's wife Evelyn in the garden. Just like in the earlier sequence, Evelyn also doesn't recognize her with her different hair color. With her high cheekbones, piercing eyes and jet-black hair, Ms. Blanchard and director Neumann have created the perfect horror antiheroine/femme fatale, but, much like Gene Tierney in John M. Stahl's *noir* thriller **LEAVE HER TO HEAVEN** (1945, USA), she is at her most devilish, duplicitous and conniving when she tries to win people over with her stunning good looks, which, simply put, hide "a devil, a creature with a warped soul"!

Upon closer inspection, Neumann's **SHE DEVIL** could, at times, be seen as a feminist picture, with Kyra, the liberated woman rebelling against the rigid and—let's face it—politically incorrect behavior of the entire male cast who, almost unwittingly, treat most of the women as mere objects. Even Dr. Scott and Dr. Bach, the "good guys" of the film, want to control her directly from the onset, when they "invite" her to stay at Bach's house, so they can keep an eye on her. But it's Archer as the Kendall character who is the epitome of the male chauvinist, who goes through women as if they're just another trophy amidst his many gun racks and hunting ephemera. Kyra is, for all intents and purposes, a "monster" that kills to get what she/it wants, but, at the very same time, it seems to be the only way to escape the grasp of this, at that time, male-dominated world.

Further ethical and philosophical discussions usually revolving around religion ensue between Dr. Scott and Dr. Bach ("We are going to put an end to this horror!") in regards to saving Kyra from a horrible death, because she was "meant to die". Despite Dr. Scott's "brilliance", Dr. Bach still regarded his drug "as a miracle", and it's his strong belief in a higher power that eventually wins over Dr. Scott and makes him realize—if maybe not wholeheartedly—the rather imprudent use of his new drug on Kyra.

Produced in-between Neumann's **KRONOS** (1957) and what is probably his best-known film, **THE FLY** (1958, both USA), **SHE DEVIL** is certainly a product of its times, which still holds up perfectly well today as undemanding Saturday morning viewing. Even though horror elements are kept to a decided minimum, there is still plenty to enjoy, including Karl Struss' rather impressive scope (2.35:1) photography, which definitely gives the entire film a bigger-budget look and feel (Struss [1886-1981] also functioned as DP on both **KRONOS** and Roy Del Ruth's **THE ALLIGATOR**

PEOPLE [1959, USA], latter of which I reviewed back in *Monster!* #12 [p.5]). Mari Blanchard (1923-1970) is also terrific, and seems to really relish portraying the "bad girl" in one of her only leading roles. Sadly, in reality, Blanchard was stricken with polio at the age of nine, which pretty much ruined her dream of becoming a dancer despite her due diligence towards her rehabilitation. Once in the Hollywood system, she had difficulty securing bigger, more prominent roles, and, tragically, she passed away from cancer in 1970. So, ironically enough, it seems that poor Ms. Blanchard could've used Dr. Scott's disease-defeating wonder drug in real life.

'50s va-va-voom vixen Mari Blanchard as Venusian Queen Allura in **ABBOTT AND COSTELLO GO TO MARS** (1953, USA)

Much like the ill-fated David Carradine (1936-2009), Albert Dekker (1905-1968) was a prolific actor who also met a mysterious and untimely end, when he was found dead in his home, hanging—handcuffed—in the shower. His final film appearance was as Harrigan in Sam Peckinpah's ultraviolent, Spaghetti-influenced "revisionist" western **THE WILD BUNCH** (1969, USA). Co-star Jack Kelly was another busy film and TV actor, who, at the time of this film's release, was enjoying a stint on the hit western teleseries *Maverick* (1957-62, USA) as Bart Maverick, alongside James Garner's title character. Italo-trash fans will recognize Kelly as Captain Valli in Armando Crispino's **DIRTY DOZEN** rip-off, **COMMANDOS** (a.k.a. **SULLIVAN'S MARAUDERS**, 1968, Italy/West Germany), wherein he was paired up with tough guy Lee Van Cleef. Although Kelly's work in monster movies came few and far between, he later—sight unseen—provided the radio announcer's voice in Stephen Traxler's **SPAWN OF THE SLITHIS** (1978, USA).

The present film had never before officially been made available on home video prior to the release of this excellent Blu-ray from Olive Films, which not only preserves Struss' original 2.35:1 photography, but the transfer looks clean, sharp and very film-like indeed. Despite some of the hokey scientific jargon heard herein, **SHE DEVIL** is a real sleeper from that highly productive era of American B-movie filmmaking, the 'Fifties.

TURN THE PAGE TO READ MORE ON THE CAPTIVATING FACTS AND FICTION BEHIND THE MAKING OF

SHE DEVIL!

ADAPTING "THE ADAPTIVE ULTIMATE"
From Print to Radio to TV to Cinema

by Les Moore

The Dr. Scott character, quoted from the story's text: *"But she isn't quite—human! ...She's not an angel but a female demon, a—what were they called?—an incubus!"*

If Looks Could Kill: The irresistibly alluring temptress Kyra Zelas (here played by Mari Blanchard) is both beauty and beast...but which is which?!

The script of Kurt Neumann's **SHE DEVIL** (1957, USA) was derived—and largely quite faithfully so, albeit with some minor additions/alterations—from celebrated Golden Age of Science Fiction author Stanley G. Weinbaum's (1902-1935) highly adaptable and oft-adapted short story "The Adaptive Ultimate" (first published under the pen name of "John Jessel" in *Astounding Stories* magazine's November 1935 issue). In addition to reappearing numerous times in subsequent other periodicals, said story *[see 1st online link below]* was reprinted in a number of different editions of Weinbaum's classic SF anthology *A Martian Odyssey*, as well as in a later collection entitled *The Best of Stanley G. Weinbaum* (Ballantine Books, 1974; reprinted by Ballantine/Del Rey in 1979. A UK paperback edition was published by Sphere Books in 1977 *[see 2nd online link below]*). Weinbaum's first and most famous story "A Martian Odyssey" was published in 1934 (in *Wonder Stories*' July issue); but, tragically, Weinbaum would be dead from lung cancer a year-and-a-half later, at the critically young age of only 33.

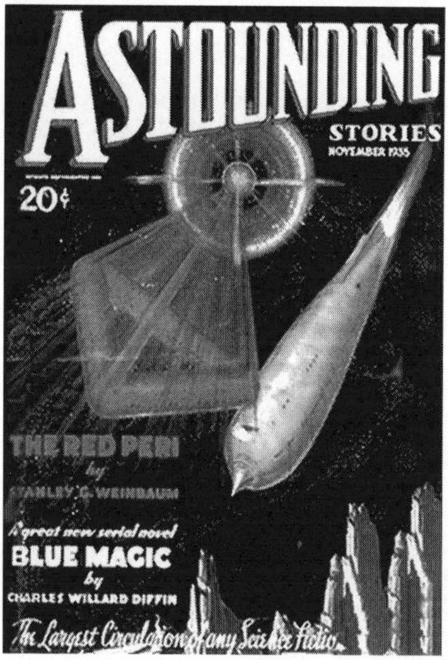

Concisely told in less than 9,000 words, the plot of "The Adaptive Ultimate" is fairly straightforward: Brilliant young biochemist Dr. Daniel Scott collaborates with his much older friend and colleague, surgeon Dr. Herman Bach, in a revolutionary medical experiment using what they hope will be a cure-all wonder drug, which they inject with her permission into the bloodstream of a terminally ill female tuberculosis sufferer, one Kyra Zelas.

In Dr. Scott's own words, regarding his scientific discovery: "...I began to look for the most adaptive of living organisms. And what are they? *Insects!* Insects, of course. Cut off a wing, and it grows back. Cut off a head, stick it to the headless body of another of the same species, and that grows back on. And what's the secret of their great adaptability? ...It's glandular, of course — a matter of hormones... There's one insect that is known to produce a higher percentage of mutants than any other, more freaks, more biological sports. The one Morgan used in his experiments on the effect of hard X-rays on heredity—the fruit fly, the ordinary fruit fly."

The injection (whose active ingredient is the hormone *pinealin*) not only saves Kyra's life, but endows her with an unnaturally-evolved, hyper-accentuated ability to physically adapt herself via instant mutation to any and all occasions, including being able to change her hair, eye and skin pigmentation—much akin to a chameleon—when required. According to Dr. Bach, "Kyra's a mutation, a jump from the human to—something else. Perhaps the superhuman." As well as bringing out her more viciously voracious, animalistic "Hyde" side, this adaptability also makes her virtually immune to destruction. No sooner than she realizes what great power she now possesses, Kyra begins misusing it to advance herself, and, when her methods become progressively more extreme, megalomaniacal and murderous, her two "creators" decide she must be stopped at all costs...

The sole dramatized adaptation to retain the story's original title, "The Adaptive Ultimate" episode (#63, March 26, 1949) of the CBS radio program *Escape* (1949-54, USA) starred Edgar "**THE GIANT CLAW**" Barrier as Dr. Herman Bach, prolific TV actor Stacy Harris as Dan Scott and Elsie Holmes as Kyra Zelas. Its script adaptation editorially supervised by one John Dunkel and with direction by Norman McDonald, this 30-minute audio dramatization *[see 3rd online link below]* at times sounds like a virtual spoken-word recording of the story; at others it veers sharply off into "creative embellishments" (including a minor witness character doing a decidedly histrionic mock-Italian accent!). One throwaway line of dialogue hints that Kyra—pronounced "Keera" in all but one of the dramatizations; although no specific pronunciation is given in Weinbaum's text—might potentially be telepathic, a detail which isn't stressed in either the original story nor any of the other versions. Here, as in the story itself, she becomes romantically entwined with John Callan, a powerfully politically-connected mover 'n' shaker in the atomic energy field, whom she hopes to use as her stepping stone/puppet in a plot to become (quote) "Empress" of the world. One of the more conspicuous additions herein is the Kyra character's habit of "seductively" (i.e., manipulatively) referring to the Scott character as "Brown Eyes"; something which she is heard to call him repeatedly during the course of

The ill-fated Stanley G. Weinbaum

the radio play, but which didn't appear in the actual source story itself. Presumably mainly because this adaptation was produced for a non-visual medium, little more than passing references are made to Kyra's chameleon-like ability to alter the color of her hair, eyes and even her skin-tone; all but the last of which were played-up to varying degrees in the video and celluloid adaptations.

The first TV adaptation, scripted by Worthington Miner and directed by Paul Nickell, was produced by CBS for Westinghouse's *Studio One in Hollywood* series (1948-58, USA). Entitled simply "Kyra Zelas" and aired on September 12, 1949, it starred Richard Hart as Dr. Dan Scott and Felicia Montealegre—a regular *Studio One* performer—as the title character, but has evidently since become lost (or at least no online sources appear to be available for it), so I can't comment about the program; although it would presumably have adhered to "Jessel"/Weinbaum's storyline quite closely.

Aired in a 30-minute timeslot—complete with two lengthy Kreisler watchband commercials—and rough-around-the-edges in the vintage live TV manner, the *Tales of Tomorrow* (1951-53, USA) episode "The Miraculous Serum" (Season 1, Episode 38, June 20, 1952 *[see 4th online link below]*) was adapted for television by SF author Theodore Sturgeon and directed by Don Medford. Richard Derr (future hero of Gerardo de Leon's **TERROR IS A MAN** [Philippines/USA, 1959]) gives an energetically enthusiastic performance as

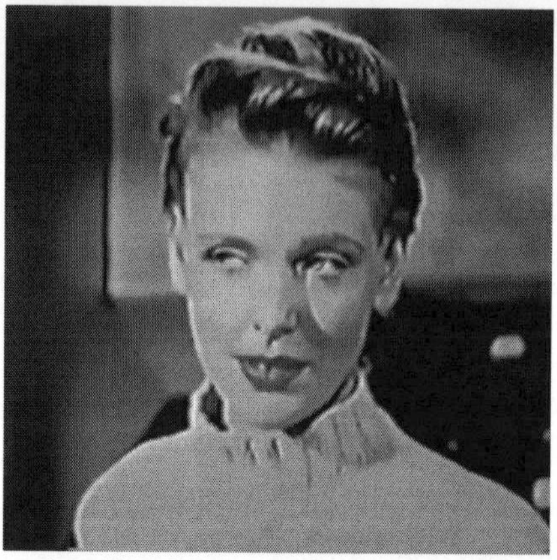

Joan Vohs in sly-eyed Kyra Zelas mode

Dr. Dan Scott, whose theories are initially soundly pooh-poohed by his senior colleague Dr. "Harry" Bach (rather awkwardly played by Louis Hector, who at one point flubs a line by conspicuously mispronouncing its operative word as "abdaptation" [*sic!*]). Yet again, a fast-ailing TB patient (herein played by Lola Albright, future heroine of **THE MONOLITH MONSTERS** [1957, USA; see *Monster!* #14, p.68]) is brought back from the brink of death by an injection of the title serum. Interestingly, this is the only one of the five dramatizations discussed here wherein the principal female character Kyra Zelas wasn't actually called that; she is here known as the far-less-exotic and more nondescript-sounding Carol Williams instead. In this much more homogenized rendition, rather than bludgeoning him to death as in the original story, our "she-devil" only non-violently lifts a man's wallet to score some easy cash. "She's the adaptive ultimate!" exclaims Dr. Bach in one of the script's numerous gross overstatements... but we ain't buying it for a second. The at times hysterical dialogue unsuccessfully—and frankly only half-heartedly—attempts to inject a sense of suspense or menace, but, even at her "nastiest" (note quotes), the too cheerful and wholesome-looking Ms. Albright never comes across as anything worse than a slightly bitchy all-American girl-next-door, possibly with mild PMS. This far from classic or even particularly interesting adaptation really carves all the guts out of Weinbaum's original story—its heart included—turning it into a bland bit of virtual nothingness whose sole plusses are the players' earnest if sometimes "off" performances. Possibly because of its potential distasteful connotations, no mention is made of fruit fly hormone being used.

The next adaptation was produced more than three years later by ZIV TV for their series *Science Fiction Theatre* (1955-57, USA). Entitled "Beyond Return" (Season 1, Episode 33, December 3, 1955 *[see 5th online link below]*), it was scripted by Doris Gilbert and directed by Eddie Davis. Regular series host Truman Bradley provided an introduction to the episode ("It has to do with a human chameleon"). This well-acted version stars Zachary Scott as Dr. Bach (whose first name became Erwin here), Peter Hansen as Dr. Dan Scott, with the high-cheekboned, lush-lipped Joan Vohs cast as Kyra Zelas. Unlike in any of the other versions—in which the pronunciation was "Keera"—Kyra's name is here pronounced to rhyme with Myra throughout. In this version, Kyra commits an off-screen nonviolent armed robbery in order to acquire some quick cash. (Much more shockingly, in the original story she at one point offhandedly admits to "accidentally" killing a small boy; a detail which—perhaps not surprisingly, considering the era—was left out of all the dramatizations.)

Her pineal gland having been enhanced/mutated by an injection of the fruit fly hormone and possessing the ability (hardly a superpower!) to change from brunette to blonde at will, in her "transformed" state she earns her living via fashion modeling, for which she physically adapts herself by becoming more beautiful than the competition, thus rising to become top in her field...but that's about as "dangerous" as she ever gets here. Despite the script informing us "She has the strength of ten!" nothing is ever done with this aspect. Wearing too much makeup, all bedroom-eyed and saucy-lipped, Vohs plays it in such a self-consciously sultry, breathy manner that she at times appears on the verge of having a fake orgasm.

In the preceding two televersions of the tale—even though she never went so far as actually physically harming anybody in the process—the mere fact that the Zelas character is an uppity goal-oriented, ruthlessly self-serving female acting-up in open defiance of the status quo (I hesitate to use the overused and simplistically inaccurate term "patriarchy") seems to be sufficient for the males who "created" her to regard her as some sort of inhuman monstrosity that must be stopped at all costs, hence the drastic measures they take to foil her plans (i.e., by returning her to her normal, "harmless" persona again). At the end of "Beyond Return", she is not only permanently changed from her conniving fair-haired alter-ego back to her "nice", meek black-haired former self again, but as a bonus remains fully cured of TB as well (said latter optimistic development isn't stressed in the original story).

And so to **SHE DEVIL** (1957, USA). As its sensationalized title implies, this the sole official cinematic version of the tale to date most accentuates the title character's more "monstrous" characteristics. The screenplay co-written by director Kurt Neumann and Carroll Young (who also co-wrote Neumann's unrelated **TARZAN AND THE SHE-DEVIL** [1953, USA], coincidentally enough) often quotes "Jessel"/Weinbaum's dialogue virtually verbatim, and the thrust and tone of the narrative remains much the same, although there are numerous little additions/subtractions made here and there (e.g., the first name of the Bach character played by Albert Dekker was changed from Herman to Richard).

Even at the outset when seen in her terminally tubercular "Before" state, Blanchard's character is clearly nowhere even close to the "drab and plain" woman described in the source story's original prose, but merely looks like a sickly beauty queen. As her "After" alter-ego, the actress' natural beauty is simply accentuated and given a more vivacious—if at times vicious—edge. With her dangerously pointy bosom (never mind just one, them things could put *both* eyes out!), wasp waist, exaggerated hip-swivel and buttocks switching provocatively from side to side in form-fitting, figure-flattering outfits, Blanchard really gets into character as the invincibly adaptable, amoral Jezebel whose charms no man can resist.

In the original story, Kyra's first murder victim is an elderly man, whom she conks over the skull with a rock in order to relieve him of his wallet in a public park. In the film, to get her hands on his dough (for the purpose of purchasing a fancy new dress, yet), Blanchard as Kyra non-fatally coldcocks an old guy with a heavy ashtray in a high-priced fashion boutique. With the greatest of ease, she can spontaneously switch her hair color from dark brunette to peroxide blonde and back again, simply by willing it to happen (I personally think Blanchard looks far hotter in her black-haired mode; but then I've never much been into blondes). The scenes in which Kyra "wills" her hair color to change were evidently accomplished in-camera, using some sort of combination of colored filters and subtly altered lighting. Even in her supposedly homely pre-treatment state, the actress still wears impeccably-applied cosmetics.

Also expanded upon is the subplot wherein, during her bid to acquire social power via sexual means, Kyra "cultivates" a multi-millionaire playboy named Barton Kendall (John Archer) right under his hoity-toity wife's very nose. The film ups the body count somewhat by having Kyra—in "dark" mode—do away with the playboy's possessive better half, whom she regards as her "romantic"

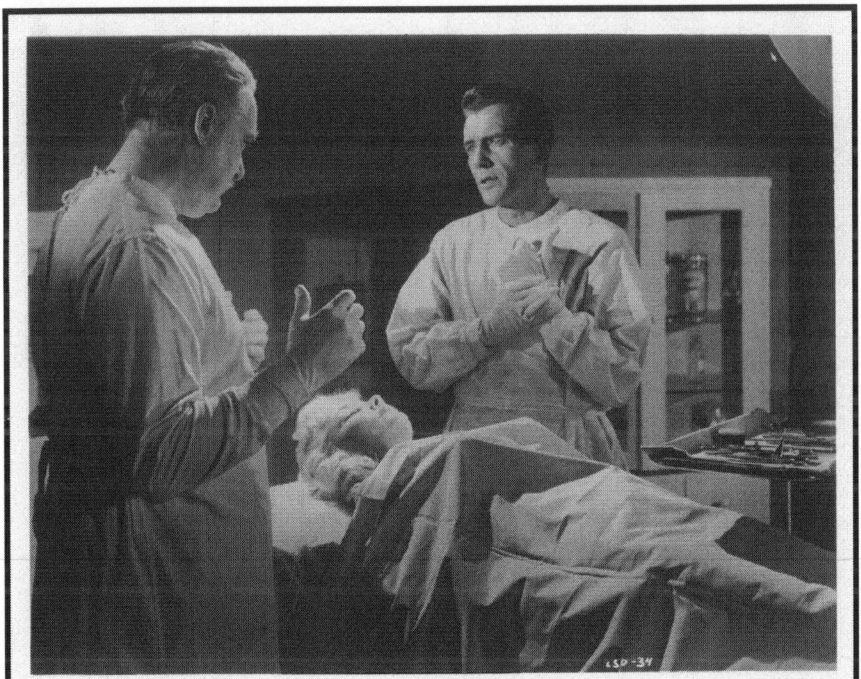

"SHE DEVIL"—20th Century-Fox Release
Printed in U.S.A.

US lobby still. Having used medical science to "create" her, doctors Bach and Scott (Albert Dekker and Jack Kelly) use it to put an end to Kyra Zelas (Mari Blanchard) in **SHE DEVIL**'s downbeat closing scenes rival while clawing her way to the top. After Kyra murders her, she and the widower Kendall tie the knot (but "wedded bliss" doesn't quite cover it, I'm afraid!).

Elsewhere, the caged black leopard in the lab—obviously symbolizing the feline Kyra's fiercely feral sexual nature ("She was so quiet and timid before")—is another dramatic elaboration, making for a decidedly Lewtonesque touch. In one scene, no sooner has she impetuously antagonized the big cat in its cage than it scratches her with its claws in retaliation; whereupon, due to her newfound instant healing capabilities, the bloody wounds completely disappear within moments. In a later scene, after taking a bullet in the shoulder, all sign of the wound vanishes without a trace in under a half-minute. She even emerges unscathed from a serious road-wreck when—no thanks to Kyra!—her hubby's sporty speedster flies off a cliff (actually footage recycled from Otto Preminger's *noir* classic **ANGEL FACE** [1952, USA], starring Robert Mitchum and Jean Simmons).

In summation, much of the "feminist" subtexts that have been read into this story over the years largely amount to hooey, as far as I'm concerned, even if it is sometimes fun reading too much into things (if anything, it's the exact opposite: a chauvinistic control fantasy which is all about keeping women in their "proper" place rather than liberating them from societal constraints; but we won't go into *that* loaded topic here! This is *Monster!* not *The Guardian*, FFS). There are plentiful holes in logic even in the original story, which stresses Kyra's potentially ravenous hunger for power more strongly than any of the other adaptations, hence justifying the scientists' harsh measures in curbing her increasingly monstrous behavior, even if their medical meddling was the direct cause of it. A mandatory "moral comeuppance" for her evil ways is tacked on at the end of the film version; one which isn't found in any of the previous versions, nor in Weinbaum's story either. You'll know it when you see it.

Lancer's 1962 US paperback edition of Weinbaum's classic SF collection, including "The Adaptive Ultimate"

All but one of the five versions discussed above are available for your entertainment (the big screen version is now extant on Blu-ray from Olive Films), so by all means check out the sites below.

NOTES: In an interesting bit of trivia, the above-covered "Beyond Return" program's assistant director was Erich von Stroheim, Jr., the son of you-know-who. In the '57 movie, appearing most ill-at-ease indeed in his spiffy white medical togs, Tod Griffin—future hero of Richard E. Cunha's analogously-titled if far schlockier **SHE DEMONS** (1958, USA [see *Weng's Chop* #4.5, p.84])—plays a supporting part as a hospital intern. Presumably merely having **SHE DEVIL** on his résumé was sufficient to earn him a co-starring role on that other gig! The latter film filled out the bill as second feature on a theatrical pair-up with Neumann's own giant robot attack classic **KRONOS**, made the same year. **THE WASP WOMAN** (1959, USA) and **THE LEECH WOMAN** (1960, USA [see *Weng's Chop* #6.5, p.29]) are only two of the films which felt the influence of "The Adaptive Ultimate" to varying degrees, either subliminally or directly.

Related links:

http://gutenberg.net.au/ebooks06/0601511h.html (PD copy of "The Adaptive Ultimate")
http://www.isfdb.org/cgi-bin/title.cgi?47548 (Bibliography for the story)
http://ia700500.us.archive.org/1/items/Escape19491950/esca.49.03.26_Adaptive_Ultimate.mp3 (*Escape* radio show episode)
http://youtube.com/watch?v=0lYQtAyNdm4 (*Tales of Tomorrow* "The Miraculous Serum" episode)
https://www.youtube.com/watch?v=ci_C3Ofc_2Y (*Science Fiction Theatre* "Beyond Return" episode)

Coming Soon...
The History of Mummies in the Movies:
Monster! International
Vol. 2 No. 1
...Watch for it!

FROM THE CHEESE RETURNED

Wither the Kings and Queens of Egypt?

by José Cruz

*Nothing inspires nostalgia quite like change. When we feel time's tectonic plates start to shift under our feet, we can't help but cast a backward glance over our shoulders, small tears collecting in our eyes as we muse, "*Oh! *But how simple it all was* back then*". In my lifetime, nothing quite flipped society's collective lid in relation to time more than the year 2000. But out of the paranoia over computer crashes and quenching heavenly fire that were inspired by the End of ~~Times~~ 1999, there arose a series of films that looked back at the world of Ancient Egypt, a civilization from several millennia ago that served as a sedative to the freaked-out masses as if to say, "See, everything turned out all right for them in the end". The fact that these films contained resurrected corpses eating humans for their insides and the worst plagues this side of the Nile was either a happy accident or an exorcism of these very fears, depending on your perspective.*

Though it came out in 1999, **THE MUMMY***—Stephen Sommers' reboot/"remake" for Universal Studios of their 1932 Karloff film—was actually preceded by two low-key productions that also sought to capitalize on the Egyptian dance craze. Looking to inject new life into the poor, sedate mummy's withered veins, they attempted to bring the shuffling schlub of the Old World into the high-speed, neon-sheen realm of the New, with varying amounts of success.*

The poster was the best thing about this earlier (1980) adaptation of Stoker's *The Jewel of Seven Stars*, starring Chuck Heston, of all people

The first, **BRAM STOKER'S THE MUMMY** (1998, USA), occupies a familiar space in the pantheon of mummy movies even with its superficial modernizing of Stoker's novel *The Jewel of Seven Stars* (1903), a book that was filmed twice prior in **BLOOD FROM THE MUMMY'S TOMB** (1971, UK, D: Seth Holt) and **THE AWAKENING** (1980, UK, D: Mike Newell). Stoker's credit is made into a dubious affair by the film, which in its end credits leads with the attribution "Written and Directed by Jeff Obrow", only to later on list Obrow, John Penney, and Lars Hauglie as the adapters with a "Based on the novel..." recognition at the bottom of the screen, but one that fails to even give Stoker's name! The very title of the film has apparently gone through a similar wringer. I recall being intrigued by the movie's VHS cover not just because it listed Stoker's name ("The guy who wrote *Dracula* did a mummy story too? *Whoa!*"), but because the box was one of those holographic deals that would show a transforming picture whenever you moved passed it. At first all I saw was the beautiful lady staring seductively at me from underneath her dirty, dirty bandages and then—*BAM!*—I got a faceful of rotten snaggletooth. Puberty was ruined.

For some reason though, the film went on to only be identified as **THE MUMMY**, as seen on the embossed labeling of the DVD, but when one tries to look it up on the IMDb, it's listed as **LEGEND**

OF THE MUMMY, which as far as marketing is concerned is at least ten steps backward. Perhaps the ghost of Florence Stoker was haunting the rights holders to have her husband's name actually *removed* from the adaptation this time around?

Whatever the case, the story of **THE MUMMY** and Stoker's novel are one in the same. A famed archaeologist (Lloyd Bochner) is attacked in his office after reading forbidden hieroglyphics, leaving him in a coma, and his daughter Margaret Trelawney (Amy Locane) with a set of instructions demanding that his body remain in the office and be constantly watched over lest a terrible fate befall them all. Amy's rugged nerd boyfriend Wyatt (Eric Lutes, who seems to be following the Stoker's dweeb-as-hero precedent set by Peter Capaldi in Ken Russell's **THE LAIR OF THE WHITE WORM** [1988, UK]) is there to help, along with a terrified staff and a chip-shouldered police sergeant (Mark Lindsay Chapman) trying to sniff out the perpetrator. Also providing pleasant cameos are British character actor Aubrey Morris—a veteran of the aforementioned **BLOOD FROM THE MUMMY'S TOMB**, as a matter of fact—and EarthLink. What they all don't realize is that the mummified remains of Queen Tera brought back from Egypt by the elder Trelawney have revived from their dusty sleep and are intent on finding renewed life in the young, supple form of Margaret. It's only when the gang enlists the aid of the slightly-crazed Corbeck (Louis Gosset, Jr.) that they begin to get a grasp on the situation, for better or worse.

Though it lacks any true innovation, **BRAM STOKER'S THE MUMMY** gets points for at least attacking its tired tropes with verve. It may bear a passing resemblance to Universal's mummy films of the '40s wherein Lon Chaney, Jr. as Kharis dragged his feet around and strangled all his victims to death. But Queen Tera gets her own sand pile in the basement where she can take a dirt nap and let all of her precious insects crawl over her face when she isn't reaching through ratty old bed frames to kill enterprising caretakers. If nothing else, Tera is a decidedly grottier mummy than the preserved museum pieces we're used to seeing in these films. And she's got a pair of rubber redneck teeth to complete the ensemble!

Obrow and his cast play the drama in earnest, but the film is still given to the snicker-inducing affectations of B-cinema. One such exchange occurs when Corbeck punctuates every word of his admonishment with a punch to Wyatt's face ("*You! Can't! Stop! This!*"), as does a bit where the mummy "preys" on Trelawney but in actuality it looks like the two are just slapping at each other's hands to call time-out, to say nothing of the "dazzling" ruby that appears to be a roughly diamond-shaped piece of solid Jell-O. Most logically egregious of

In **BRAM STOKER'S THE MUMMY**, respected thespian Louis Gossett, Jr. wonders how the hell he got stuck with using such cheesy props

US DVD cover

THE CURSE IS LEGEND. THE ADVENTURE IS REAL.
RUSSELL MULCAHY'S
TALE OF
THE MUMMY
DVD

US DVD cover

all is when a PI sent by Chapman's police sergeant to dig around Corbeck's office is apparently attacked by the mummy's curse. We see the office spontaneously catch on fire and the actor thrash and scream around like his SAG card depended on it…only for him to show up in a later scene with a bandaged scratch on his cheek. Somebody must have been carrying their rabbit's foot that day! Even when Sergeant Daw sinks into the cellar sand pit and has cockroaches crawl on him, he suffers the less embarrassing fate compared to Wyatt, who gets his hand stuck in an old mummy crotch and has to ask Corbeck for help.

For all of that, the movie isn't really that bad. The middle section does sag, but it's not so much from lack of exciting events as from lackluster direction that fails to stir sufficient tension from those events. The cinematography and set design are appropriately musty with their accentuation of deep browns and dusty golds. The film also boasts practical effects that lend it a certain charm and make it more seem a closer descendant of the older mummy films. Obrow even manages to bring the story to a satisfying close. The transmutation scene is cleverly handled, showing Margaret holding the remains of Queen Tera in between bursts of light, creating a strobe effect that allows the mummy to disappear in a flash and show the now-possessed Margaret exult in her victory. This results in the "shocking" epilogue being not so shocking, but it's delivered with a good, ominous beat that makes its inclusion more than forgivable. Obrow clearly wanted to have his cake and eat it too, and that's fine.

But the pinnacle came during a nightmare sequence in which my own time-traveling frissons were relived with all too much clarity. While Wyatt and one of his colleagues (Richard Karn of *Home Improvement* fame) discuss the nature of the curse at Trelawney's mansion, they're alerted by a thumping sound coming from a small sarcophagus in the corner of the bedroom. Upon opening it, they see a diminutive corpse—perhaps that of a child—wrapped in moldering gauze. Suddenly, the body leaps forth and tackles Karn to the ground, snapping off his fingers with a crunching noise like so many dead tana leaves being ground underfoot, as the man screams and Wyatt looks on in frozen terror. Soon Karn is fingerless on one hand, his face turned into a sandy, dried husk. Wyatt races back to the bed to awaken Margaret, only to find a skull leering back at him. It was at this point that my mind screamed out "*YOU'VE SEEN THIS BEFORE!*" and all of the fear that I had watching this scene as a traumatized child came rushing back to me as I remembered how utterly disturbed I was by that short, squealing corpse. When I heard those crunches, I knew that the mummy kid was going to get me when he jumped out from the darkness of my closet and do the same thing. *Snap, snap*, one by one. Squealing the whole time. Sometimes the tears that develop in our eyes from looking back at the past are for entirely different reasons.

***

Russell Mulcahy, the director from the Outback who gained fame with popular music videos for Duran Duran and cult classics such as **RAZORBACK** (1984, Australia [see *Monster!* #2, p.15]), **HIGHLANDER** (1986, UK), and **THE SHADOW** (1994, USA), brought his action-geared sensibility to the Egyptian revenant story with **TALE OF THE MUMMY** (1998, USA/UK/Germany). Mulcahy and co-screenwriter John Esposito tried to give the long-dead emperor a set of flashy new clothes to ensure that the sophisticated audiences on the cusp of the terrifying new millennium would take note of its style and not its staleness.

Compared to **BRAM STOKER'S THE MUMMY**, Mulcahy's picture certainly looks like an impressive product on paper just by the list of participants. With a cast including a mix of soon-to-be familiar faces (Gerard Butler and Sean Pertwee, whose raspy London accent and chiseled looks make him and Mark Lindsay Chapman from the former film a pair of dead ringers), prolific character actors (Mi-

Roger W. Morrissey as the mummy and Louise Lombard as the mama in **TALE OF THE MUMMY**

chael Lerner), industry veterans (Christopher Lee, Honor Blackman, Shelley Duvall), and treasured Generation Y action hero (Jason Scott Lee), along with special makeup provided by the venerated gore gurus at KNB Effects (*The Walking Dead*), production design by Simon Bowles (**THE DESCENT**, 2005, UK, D: Neil Marshall) and cinematography by Gabriel Beristain (**BLADE II**, 2002, USA/Germany, D: Guillermo del Toro), **TALE OF THE MUMMY** was clearly not the product of amateurs and unproven schmucks.

And yet…

They say you can't teach an old dog new tricks, and sometimes you *shouldn't*. Whatever his other deficits might be, Stephen Sommers was canny enough to understand what it was that made the mummy terrifying as a character and accentuated those qualities in his film as opposed to trying to replace those assets with a whole new set of magic tricks, which is what Mulcahy tries doing here. (For the record, I enjoy Sommers' film quite a bit.)

We can almost tell from the start what kind of picture this is going to be. After we see Christopher Lee's Sir Richard Turkel—the leader of the archaeological team defiling the sacred earth this time around—and his comrades eat it in a bad way when their plundering gets them facefuls of noxious tomb-fumes that cause their bodies to crumble away, we see present-day explorers suited up like the crew of the *Nostromo* as they excavate the burial ground. Further "novelty" is added when we see that the buried pharaoh, Talos, was so especially evil that he couldn't be interred in your average upright sarcophagus but had to be suspended from the ceiling in an egg-shaped casket over a pit of spears so that none could disturb his unholy slumber. Gerard Butler tries doing so in an attempt to fetch a pretty talisman as an "engagement ring" for his girlfriend before he himself is among the impaled. We find out later that Talos was indeed a sordid sort, the type of ruler who enjoyed using his power for the facilitation of copious torture and blood-filled chalice-drinking.

A mummy too big for his wrappings, you'd say. And you'd be right.

For when the long-dead prince breaks free from his new home as an exhibit at the British museum, it's his sentient bandages that do all the dirty work, writhing and flying through the air to attack his prey like so many desert snakes to lay claim to their juicy organs before the planets align. The irony here is that Mulcahy and Esposito's thinking must have been that the sight of the sheathed, creeping mummy would have been much too tame and old-fashioned for their sophisticated viewers, so they decided to improve the formula by showing people screaming through a ball of gauze that can form itself into a fist which can punch through windows and transform into harmless dogs to fool its victims.

Spoiler: it's not very scary.

Mulcahy seems to realize the inherent silliness of what he's trying to pull off, perhaps no more clearly seen than when a poor sap in a men's bathroom tries using the towel dispenser to dry his face only to get an armful of bandages that drag him shrieking into one of the stalls and down the toilet. (This is preceded by one of my all-time movie soft spots, the '90s dance club scene!) The director intersperses these jocular moments with homages to genre classics (a victim hearing a sonorous voice in a parking garage recalls **CANDYMAN** [1992, USA, D: Bernard Rose] and the gratuitous POV shots of a blind man's seeing-eye dog in the London Underground have a flavoring of **AN AMERICAN WEREWOLF IN LONDON** [1981, USA/UK, D: John Landis]), but his mishandling of the material leads scenes that should be at least halfway-serious—like the séance where Pertwee's dead loony revives to point the heroes in the direction of the marauding mummy, for instance—to become limply-acted excursions into the absurd.

The apotheosis of the laughably puzzling elements at work here is Jason Scott Lee's character, Detective Riley. When the whispery investigator arrives on the scene of the first homicide at the museum, he immediately begins hypothesizing the work of a serial killer. When they go to question Pertwee at his apartment and knock on the door, Riley has his gun ready and aimed for the perp to answer. At a tavern, Turkel's granddaughter Samantha (Louise Lombard) confides with Riley in a moment of honesty about the disturbing madness that overcame their expedition, to which his sage response is to take away her glass and say, "You're cut off".

Given how the story ends, this could just possibly be a case of clever misdirection. But one reveal is enough for this column, so I'm afraid you'll have to seek this one out if you are truly interested in seeing how it turns out. Not a difficult task, given that the film is available on Netflix's streaming service. You won't have to count on getting the VHS as a Christmas present as I did, wondering if the image of the bound cadaver under the cross-hatching of sand and dust would "live up" to my expectations. **TALE OF THE MUMMY** is one of those studio-sanctioned curiosities that somehow manages to be even cheesier, or just cheesy as, than the work of lower-budgeted efforts like **BRAM STOKER'S THE MUMMY**. It only goes further to prove that cheese comes in all forms, from the pricy delicacy to the fifty-cent mass production. When the Hollywood picture is the one using stock screams and library cues more unabashedly than the independent feature, it's only easier to tell which cheese is which.

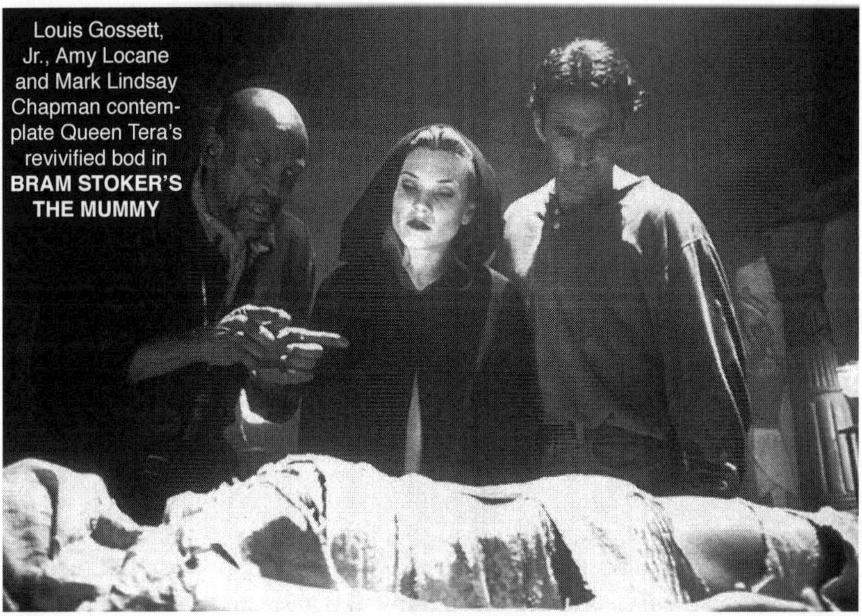

Louis Gossett, Jr., Amy Locane and Mark Lindsay Chapman contemplate Queen Tera's revivified bod in **BRAM STOKER'S THE MUMMY**

NEXT ISSUE:
An alluring publicity pose of Elisabeth Brooks, taken to promote Joe Dante's **THE HOWLING**, a film that will be covered in Troy Howarth's "My Favorite Lycanthropes" (pt. 2).

MY FAVORITE LYCANTHROPES (Pt. 1)

by Troy Howarth

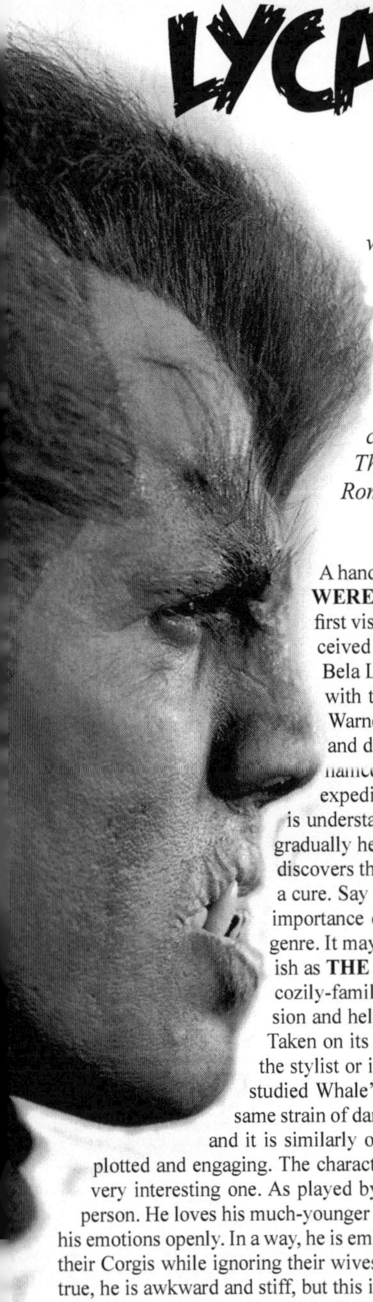

There is something particularly fascinating about the werewolf myth, especially to young boys. The reasons for this are obvious: werewolf mythology deals with body transmogrification and usually pertains to otherwise-innocent protagonists who do not understand what is happening to them. It's a pretty on-the-nose metaphor for puberty, in fact, even if many of the kids salivating over the cool man-to-beast transformations in the cinema can't quite put their finger on the true source of its appeal. The werewolf myth can be traced back at least as far as the Roman Empire, but it took a while for a real honest-to-goodness "wolf man" to be depicted on the screen.

A handful of silent films allude to the condition, but it was the release of **WEREWOLF OF LONDON** (1935, USA) which provided the screen's first visualization of a man transforming into a werewolf. Originally conceived as a vehicle for Universal's genre superstars Boris Karloff and Bela Lugosi, the film underwent some changes and ultimately emerged with the far less-beloved (by genre fans, at any rate) Henry Hull and Warner Oland in the lead roles. Written by John Colton (1887-1946) and directed by Stuart Walker (1888-1941), the film tells of a biologist named Wilfred Glendon (Hull) who is bitten by a werewolf while on an expedition in Tibet. Returning to polite society life in London, Glendon is understandably panic-stricken when he blacks out during the full moon; gradually he comes to realize that he has been infected with lycanthropy and discovers that his attacker, Dr. Yogami (Oland), is also in London looking for a cure. Say what one will about the finished product, there is no denying the importance of **WEREWOLF OF LONDON** in the evolution of the horror genre. It may not have been executed with quite the same "A" production polish as **THE BRIDE OF FRANKENSTEIN** (1935, USA) or offer one of the cozily-familiar genre stars in the title role, but the film still made an impression and helped to pave the way for countless subsequent werewolf pictures. Taken on its own terms, there is much to admire here. Director Walker is not the stylist or innovator that James Whale (1889-1957) had been, but he clearly studied Whale's output in preparing this picture. The film is informed with the same strain of dark (sometimes farcical) humor which dominated Whale's pictures, and it is similarly ornate in its set dressings and art direction. The story is cleverly plotted and engaging. The character of Glendon, often dismissed as a pissy cold fish, is actually a very interesting one. As played by Hull (1890-1977), Glendon is a brilliant but socially awkward person. He loves his much-younger wife, Lisa (Valerie Hobson [1917-1998]), but is unable to express his emotions openly. In a way, he is emblematic of the type of stiff-upper-lipped Englishmen who dote on their Corgis while ignoring their wives. To suggest that Glendon is unsympathetic is missing the point: true, he is awkward and stiff, but this is deliberate. His pent-up emotions give rise to some very moving moments, especially when he locks himself away in an abandoned building hoping to save Lisa from possibly being attacked. Walker stages the action beautifully and there's a real doozy of a transformation scene which is properly singled-out for praise by many reviewers; utilizing traveling matte technology perfected for Whale's **THE INVISIBLE MAN** (1933, USA), it follows Glendon as he moves from his den to the laboratory, his appearance changing radically as he moves, each stage of the makeup concealed by a cut as he passes behind various pillars. It's a remarkably ambitious and sophisticated bit of technical wizardry for what was, in essence, a B picture. Nothing else quite compares to it, arguably, but the film still moves at a brisk pace and holds up beautifully over many repeat viewings. Unfortunately, the film came at an awkward time in Universal's horror production schedule—outrage over the excesses of films like Lew Landers' **THE RAVEN** (1935, USA) and aforementioned **THE BRIDE OF FRANKENSTEIN** sent the British Board of Film Censors into a puritanical tailspin, and a ban was instituted on importing horror movies. Sooner than lose out on a big chunk of the English-speaking market, Universal ended up putting the kibosh on the horror cycle after a pair of stylish and often-underrated contributions from B-western specialist Lambert Hillyer: **DRACULA'S DAUGHTER** and **THE INVISIBLE RAY** (both 1936, USA).

It took a couple of years for the studio to revisit the werewolf mythos once it got back on macabre track with Rowland V. Lee's **SON OF FRANKENSTEIN** (1939, USA), but when it finally happened, a new icon was introduced. **THE WOLF MAN** (1941, USA) was an original screenplay by Curt Siodmak (1902-2000), and it ignored most of the mythology laid down in **WEREWOLF OF LONDON**. In place of an emotionally stunted protagonist, it offers a "regular guy" for the purposes of audience identification: Lawrence ("call me Larry") Talbot, played by Lon Chaney, Jr., is a big lug who spent his formative years in America before he is called back to Wales (or rather, Hollywood's vision of it) to attend the funeral of his late brother. Viewers who felt that Hull's Glendon was a little too stodgy and reserved had no such qualms about Talbot. Indeed, the Talbot character lays the symbolic underpinnings of the werewolf mythology even more bare for the audience. The ultimate outsider figure, he is well-meaning but clumsy and out of place in the proper society he finds himself inserted into, and even his attempts at wooing a local cutie (played by scream queen Evelyn Ankers [1918-1985]) are stymied because she's already engaged to a smoother, more conventionally handsome man (Patric Knowles [1911-1995]). He's a bit old to fit the bill of the "adolescent grappling with body dysmorphia" angle, but it is the symbolism that counts. Chaney, who was born as Creighton Tull Chaney and spent the early part of his career trying to distance himself from the legacy of his famous father, was born in 1906. By most accounts, his childhood was not exactly a bed of roses, but he defied his father's wishes that he should go in to anything but acting and found himself essaying a variety of thug roles in serials and B-westerns in the 1930s. The tide turned in 1939 when he convinced director Lewis Milestone to give him a chance at playing the role of Lennie in his planned screen version of Steinbeck's novel *Of Mice and Men* (1937). Chaney had already played the role on stage and knew that he could deliver; Milestone was impressed and duly cast the young actor in the role, opposite Burgess Meredith (1907-1997) as George. Chaney won a lot of praise for his sensitive performance but was—amazingly—snubbed for an Oscar nomination. It didn't exactly result in a stream of enticing offers for subsequent film work, but **OF MICE AND MEN** did get the actor noticed.

"*The Human Wolf*": A contemporaneous Hispanic newspaper ad for **WEREWOLF OF LONDON**. The same Spanish title was also applied to 1941's **THE WOLF MAN** for some Latin-American releases

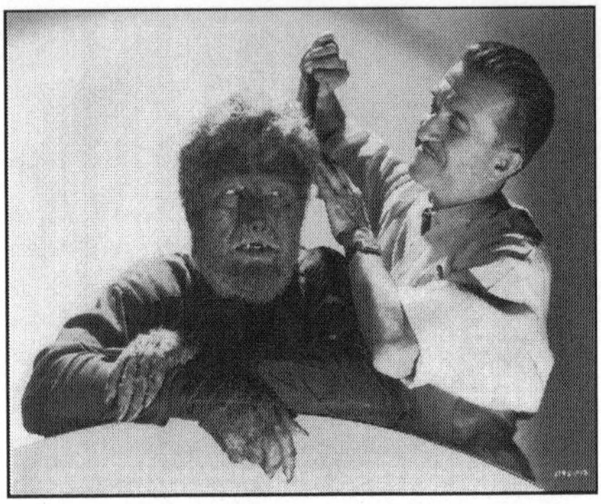

Chaney, Jr. and makeup maestro Jack P. Pierce, behind-the-scenes

Within a couple of years, Chaney found himself under contract to Universal, who initially cast him as another well-meaning lug who finds himself turned into a monster by mad scientist Lionel Atwill (1885-1946) in **MAN MADE MONSTER** (1941, USA). The film was directed by George Waggner (1894-1984), who ended up inheriting the far more prestigious assignment of helming **THE WOLF MAN**, as well. **THE WOLF MAN** transformed Chaney into a bona fide star, though Universal's attempts at selling him as their new "master character actor" resulted in the actor being shoehorned into many roles for which he was ill-suited. Fans continue to debate his merits as an actor, but, seen outside of the genre in character roles for the likes

Poster for the 1963 Italian rerelease of **FRANKENSTEIN MEETS THE WOLFMAN** (art unsigned)

of Fred Zinnemann's **HIGH NOON** (1952, USA) and Stanley Kramer's **THE DEFIANT ONES** (1958, USA), it is clear that he was ideally suited to essaying good-hearted secondary characters. Chaney's struggles with alcoholism are well-documented, and by the 1960s he found himself relegated to appearing in no-budget trash like David L. Hewitt's **GALLERY OF HORROR** (1967, USA) in order to pay the bills. Chaney's father had been cut down in his prime by throat cancer, but this didn't stop Junior from smoking like a chimney, as well. He developed cancer, as well, and his final screen appearance—in Al Adamson's awful **DRACULA VS. FRANKENSTEIN** (1971, USA [see *Monster!* #6, p.62])—was all the more depressing because he could no longer speak and looked terribly bloated due to years of alcohol abuse. He died in 1973.

There's no denying that Larry Talbot, a.k.a. The Wolf Man, is Chaney's most enduring and iconic screen role; he would even refer to it as his "baby". He is at his best in this initial instalment, but, sadly, the character's morbid desire for self-destruction would make him come off as whiny and annoying in subsequent entries. Chaney holds his own against a remarkably accomplished supporting cast, and if one has a hard time believing that the 6' 2"-tall actor could have sprung from the loins of 5' 6" Claude Rains (1889-1967), cast as his screen father, it pays to remember that Chaney Senior was only 5' 7"; that said, the originally-cast Basil Rathbone (1892-1967), who stood at 6' 1", would have seemed more evenly-matched onscreen. In any event, Chaney and Rains convey great chemistry together: Chaney is boisterous and oh-so-American, while the veddy British Rains seems by turns bemused and touched by his "son's" manner of expression. The finale of the film, in which Rains is forced to kill Chaney, is still very potent; the look of sheer horror and disbelief on Rains' face when the creature turns back to human form is simply magnificent. **THE WOLF MAN** is not without its flaws—the fact that Talbot always wears the same suit of clothes when he changes into the werewolf is peculiar, to say the least, and the bit where the character walks out of frame on tip toe is more likely to provoke snickers than shudders—but it remains one of the studio's most beloved horror films. It's not in the same tier as, say, James Whale's classics of the 1930s or Edgar G. Ulmer's perverse and masterful **THE BLACK CAT** (1934, USA), but it is certainly the best of the Talbot adventures; the entries which came in its wake seem pretty tepid by comparison.

Once the Universal horror cycle waned and ended in the inevitable self-destruction of parody—in the form of Charles T. Barton's charming **ABBOTT AND COSTELLO MEET FRANKENSTEIN**

(1948, USA), the last film to feature Chaney as Talbot—the genre lay mostly dormant until Hammer Films picked up the torch and ran with it in the UK. Having already turned their attentions to Frankenstein, Dracula and The Mummy, they inevitably made their acquaintance with the werewolf in 1961. **THE CURSE OF THE WEREWOLF** tells the story of a servant girl (Yvonne Romain, born in 1938) who is raped by a beggar (Richard Wordsworth [1915-1993]) and gives birth to a bastard child on Christmas Day. The child, named Leon and adopted by a well-to-do gentleman (Clifford Evans [1912-1985]), is raised in a loving environment—but when he grows into adulthood and goes into the world, Leon (Oliver Reed [1938-1999]), succumbs to the temptations of the flesh and feels the stirring of the beast within. The literate screenplay was written by producer Anthony Hinds (1922-2013) under the pen-name of John Elder in a bid to save some money on hiring a screenwriter; he discovered that he had a natural flair for writing scripts and would go on to write some of Hammer's most intriguing scenarios, including **THE REPTILE** (1966, UK) and **TASTE THE BLOOD OF DRACULA** (1970, UK). The script was based on the novel *The Werewolf of Paris*, written by Guy Endore (1901-1970) and published in 1933. The setting was instead switched to Spain so that Hammer could make use of some sets constructed for a proposed thriller about the Spanish Inquisition which got scuttled thanks to too many objections from the censors. The end result has the structure and feel of a mini-epic, spanning a number of years and encompassing some very pointed sociopolitical commentary.

The real villain is not the werewolf in this instance; instead, it is the depraved aristocracy, represented by the irresistibly named Marques Siniestro, played to slimy perfection by Anthony Dawson (1916-1992). It is the Marques who sets the tragedy in motion by imprisoning the poor beggar for his own twisted amusement, which causes the man's mental state to deteriorate over the years until he is reduced to a sort of pathetic animal himself. The Marques' foul temper and insatiable desire for every vice known to mankind results in his developing syphilis, a factor which Hinds could not at that time explicitly discuss in the dialogue, but which is artfully conveyed via the rather repulsive makeup designed by Hammer's in-house makeup guru Roy Ashton (1909-1995). The Marques turns his lustful attentions to the servant girl, who is thrown in the dungeon for failing to comply with his wishes; it is there that she is raped by the beggar, who succumbs to heart failure as a result of his amorous exertions. The offspring of this attack is cursed from the get-go, but it is not exactly the Catholic Church which is to blame. Some viewers have overzealously suggested that **THE CURSE OF THE WEREWOLF** was an assault on the Church, but the film does not really support such a reading. Hinds and director Terence Fisher (1904-1980) were not Catholic themselves, and it seems unlikely that they had a particular stake in lobbing insults at the Church. Indeed, the representative

AVON
A WEIRD NOVEL ABOUT A MONSTER-WOLF IN HUMAN FORM
THE WEREWOLF OF PARIS
GUY ENDORE

1950s US paperback edition (art unsigned)

Scary Hairy: Lycanthrope Oliver Reed, in all his gory glory, suffers **THE CURSE OF THE WEREWOLF**

In this US lobby card, howlin' wolfboy Oliver Reed menaces busty fox Yvonne Romain, who is showing a lot less cleavage here than she did in other promotional stills released in conjunction with the film

of the church in the film is a kindly—if ineffectual—priest (John Gabriel [1914-1998]), who embodies the best qualities of empathy and kindness throughout. One could argue that the superstitious belief that children born on Christmas Day are seen as an insult to God Almighty is indicative of a petty and even vile deity figure, but the fact of the matter is that the problems stem from a corrupt aristocracy, symbolized by the syphilitic Marques. This

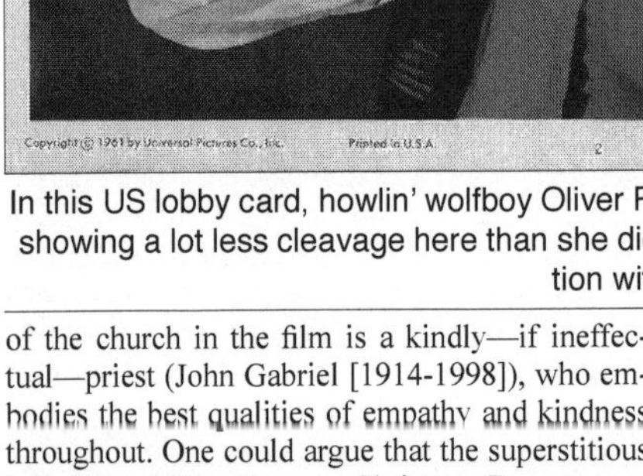

A panel of John Bolton's art from a comics adaptation of **CURSE** which ran in *House of Horror* magazine (#1, 1978)

is consistent with the sociopolitical commentary evident in many Hammer films, especially those written by Hinds. The role of the Church in this is incidental by comparison; the priest offers words of comfort and advice, but is unable to help—but this is not enough in itself to support the reading that the film is looking to attack or undermine the Church in any way, shape or form. Truth be told, Hammer's screenwriters were not always exactly subtle, so if that were really what Hinds and Fisher had had in mind, they likely would have made the priest character a far less sympathetic figure.

No matter how one chooses to interpret it, however, **THE CURSE OF THE WEREWOLF** is essential Hammer. Fisher's direction is typically assured, with great emphasis on character and emotion. Some viewers have complained that there is far too little werewolf action, but I would argue that the emphasis on build-up is essential to the film's impact; and the payoff at the end, when Leon is finally revealed in full werewolf form, is more than worth it. Ashton's makeup is probably his finest work ever: the design is closer to the vaguely "satanic" design by Jack Pierce for **WEREWOLF OF LONDON** than the more dog-like visage created by Pierce for Chaney in **THE WOLF MAN** and its sequels. Combined with Reed's ferocious and energetic performance, this makes Leon a very frightening monster indeed; but as is typical with Fisher, the humanity beneath the exterior is never lost, and the final image of tears streaming down the creature's face when he is felled by a bullet from his loving stepfather has been known to produce a lump in the throat. Reed, whose career more or less got its start at Hammer, relishes his first starring role; it's not his best performance by any means, but it shows remarkable strength and discipline for such a young (and basically untrained) performer. Within a few years, he would go on to become a major star under the tutelage of directors like Michael Winner (1935-2013) and Ken Russell (1927-2011), but, like Chaney before him, he would become as well-known for his problems with alcoholism. A beloved "hellraiser", Reed was on the cusp of a major comeback thanks to a plum supporting role in Ridley Scott's epic **GLADIATOR** (2000, USA/UK), but he died during production of a massive heart attack following an epic night of drinking at a bar on location Malta, and his role had to be completed with the aid of CGI trickery. He remains one of England's most compelling actors, and he may well be, for this writer anyway, the finest and most convincing werewolf the screen has ever seen. Unfortunately, **THE CURSE OF THE WEREWOLF** was not quite as successful at the box office as Hammer's Dracula, Frankenstein and Mummy adventures had proved to be, so they would never revisit the werewolf mythology again. Indeed, werewolves in British cinema would prove to be a little scarce altogether, though there would be some exceptions.

Probably the best and most memorable of the "other" British werewolf adventures emerged in 1965 thanks to Hammer's chief competitor, Amicus Productions. Formed by Americans abroad Max J. Rosenberg (1914-2004) and Milton Subotsky (1921-1991), Amicus—the name means "friend" in Latin—started off making mostly rock-and-roll pictures, but diehard horror and fantasy buff Subotsky soon steered the ship into the muddy waters of the horror genre. Truth be told, Subotsky had a major bone to pick with Hammer, and was only too ready and willing to offer them some stiff competition: he had submitted a screenplay to Hammer in the 1950s for a proposed remake of **FRANKENSTEIN**, but Anthony Hinds and his associates dismissed the script as unusable. Even so, some elements reportedly worked their way into the screenplay penned by Jimmy Sangster (1927-2011) for **THE CURSE OF FRANKENSTEIN** (1957, UK [see *M!* #13, p.11]), the film which basically put Hammer on the map and established them as Britain's specialists in the macabre. Subotsky took the theft—be it real or imagined—to heart and never missed a chance to dismiss or disparage Hammer's output in interviews. Even so, he

Spoiler Alert! Ursula Howells as the—*er*—"werewolf" woman in **DR. TERROR'S HOUSE OF HORRORS**

recognized that the people they used in their films had box office cachet as well as a flair for delivering quality on a budget, so for **DR. TERROR'S HOUSE OF HORRORS** (UK, 1965) he borrowed such Hammer veterans as actors Peter Cushing (1913-1994), Christopher Lee (born 1922), Michael Gough (1916-2011), director Freddie Francis (1917-2007), makeup artist Roy Ashton, composer Elisabeth Lutyens (1906-1983), and cinematographer Alan Hume (1924-2010).

Eschewing the Gothic trappings of Hammer, Subotsky decided to make his horror films mostly in the modern era—and quite a few, including **DR. TERROR**, would reuse the portmanteau format utilized in Ealing Studios' **DEAD OF NIGHT** (1945, UK), one of the producer's favorite films. Taking a cue from Hinds, Subotsky also elected to write many of the scripts himself, though his own scenarios were seldom as creative or well-developed as those of his competitor. **DR. TERROR** tells of a group of passengers aboard a train who have their fortunes read to them by the mysterious Dr. Schreck (Cushing). The first segment deals with an architect (Neil McCallum [1929-1976]) who goes to his ancestral home and comes face-to-face with a werewolf. It's a slim story and it doesn't get a hell of a lot of screen time, but director Francis imbues the segment—simply titled "Werewolf"—with an air of doom and gloom. The would-be sting-in-the-tail ending is obvious from a mile away, but no matter: "Werewolf" moves at a fast clip and delivers where it really counts. Francis, who established himself as one of England's finest cinematographers before embarking on a career as a director, was never a big fan of the horror genre. He never gave his films the sense of gravity and tragedy that Fisher imbued in his scenarios, but his early works, including **DR. TERROR**, are distinguished by a playful streak and a capacity for making something stylish out of the most unpromising of scenarios. "Werewolf" is a key example of this in his filmography. In the hands of a lesser director—or even in the hands of Francis beyond the 1970s, when his annoyance over being typed as a horror director manifested itself in some shockingly bad work—the segment would have been nothing but a trifle, but Francis makes it work. Hume's colorful widescreen photography is at times reminiscent of what Mario Bava (1914-1980) was doing in Italy, and Lutyens' music helps to create a sense of suspense where the material does not. Amicus would revisit the werewolf story only one more time, with Paul Annett's **THE BEAST MUST DIE** (1974, UK), but for all its merits—and I would argue there are many—it is let down by possibly the lamest werewolf in screen history. That is a film to be discussed at another time, however, as I cannot in good conscience include it among a survey of my *favorite* lycanthropes!

The next big "thing" in werewolves was undoubtedly the emergence of Jacinto Molina, a.k.a. Paul Naschy, as Spain's first real horror star (see *M!* #8, pp.38-55). Born in Madrid in 1934, Molina became a lifelong fan of the macabre thanks to a childhood screening of Roy William Neill's **FRANKENSTEIN MEETS THE WOLF MAN** (1943, USA), the first of the Talbot sequels. Molina established himself as a champion weightlifter and bodybuilder, but he yearned to convey his passion for horror on screen. His imposing build secured him some minor roles in a number of films, but he was more interested in writing than in performing. He wrote a screenplay about a Polish nobleman who falls under the curse of the werewolf and originally had hopes of attracting Lon Chaney, Jr. to star. However, by the time the script was optioned for production it was determined that Chaney's health was too precarious, and a search was instigated for a new actor. Eventually the producers approached Molina with the idea of starring; he was taken aback, but decided that he was willing to take the risk. As was so often the case in the Euro horror scene, the producer had their eye on selling the film to America and Great Britain, so Molina was encouraged to come up with an Anglo pseudonym as an actor, though he was allowed to sign the script under his own name. Thus, Paul Naschy made his debut—in a scenario written by Jacinto Molina—in *La marca del Hombre Lobo*, or **THE MARK OF THE WOLF MAN** (1968, Spain/West Germany). The film proved to be a success and was picked up for American distribution by Sam Sherman (born 1940) of the infamous Independent-International (I-I) company. Looking to satisfy a contractual obligation for a Frankenstein movie, he concocted a ridiculous animated prologue in which it is explained that the Frankenstein family was afflicted with lycanthropy, and Sherman thereafter retitled the film **FRANKENSTEIN'S BLOODY TERROR**.

US tie-in novelization for **WEREWOLF SHADOW**, under its better-known alternate title

Naschy was on his way to becoming a minor name in the international horror scene, but it took a few years before he really broke out in a meaningful way. The moment of truth, so to speak, presented itself in 1970 when Naschy collaborated with Argentinian director León Klimovsky on **WEREWOLF SHADOW** (*La noche de Walpurgis*, Spain/West Germany). The film was actually the fourth instalment in the Daninsky saga, following the unfinished "NIGHTS OF THE WEREWOLF" (*Las noches del Hombre Lobo*, 1968, Spain/France) and **ASSIGNMENT TERROR** (*Los monstruos del terror*, 1969, Spain/West Germany/Italy), but **WEREWOLF SHADOW** would prove to be the first to really make it as an international success. It is also arguably the best of the Daninsky films, though individual taste will vary. The story deals with a couple of girls who become stranded on the Daninsky estate while searching

Promotional still from **THE NIGHT OF THE WEREWOLF** (*El retorno del Hombre Lobo*, 1980)
Naschy's 8th (technically 9th) outing as the cursed nobleman Waldemar Daninsky

for the tomb of the infamous vampire Countess Wandesa Dárvula de Nadasdy (Patty Shepard [1945-2013]). Waldemar (Naschy, of course) comes to their aid and shows them the burial place of the Countess, who is then accidentally revived. Released in the US as **THE WEREWOLF VS. THE VAMPIRE WOMAN**, this is an essential Spanish horror item. Director Klimovsky was a jack-of-all-genres who came to the horror genre late in his life, but he showed a certain flair for this sort of material. Much of the film is handled in a fairly competent if unimaginative fashion, but the horror set-pieces are staged with great flair and even a dash of poetry. Klimovsky uses slow-motion to create some dreamy effects, though Naschy would later claim that this idea was specified in his screenplay. No matter whose idea, it works very well indeed. The assorted attacks and confrontations are appropriately eerie and well-done and the makeup on Daninsky's werewolf is much better than it had been in earlier installments. Naschy's performance is also much stronger here, especially compared to his somewhat wooden turn in **THE MARK OF THE WOLF MAN**. It is clear that greater experience resulted in greater confidence in Naschy's screen presence, and within a few years he would develop into a truly talented character actor. **WEREWOLF SHADOW** is not without its moments of ineptitude, but overall it's a remarkably confident and well-made little movie. The use of actual castles and locales aids the film's atmosphere, and it's truly the sort of film that is wonderful to revisit after an exasperating day in the dreaded "real world". The film's success helped to transform Naschy into a viable genre star, and he would eventually add the role of director to his roster of roles, as well. He would continue to revisit the Daninsky character in films of his own creation until 1987's self-reflexive **HOWL OF THE DEVIL** (*El aullido del diablo*, Spain), while schlock filmmaker Fred Olen Ray (born 1954) would resurrect the character and bring an ailing Naschy onboard to play it one last time in the well-intended but hopelessly inept softcore sex-and-horror romp **THE UNLIVING**, or **THE TOMB OF THE WEREWOLF**, in 2004. Rightly proud of his achievements and looking towards the future in the hopes of continuing to bring a touch of the Gothic to Spanish cinema, Naschy succumbed to cancer in 2009.

The werewolf genre then came to its apotheosis with a stunning one-two punch in 1981. Two directors known as much for comedy as for horror would unleash two different but tonally similar werewolf films that fateful year. Part 2 of this highly subjective overview will seek to answer the age-old question: Which is the better werewolf film: John Landis' **AN AMERICAN WEREWOLF IN LONDON** or Joe Dante's **THE HOWLING**?

I hope you'll join me next issue, when I attempt to sort my own feelings out on *that* particular dilemma!

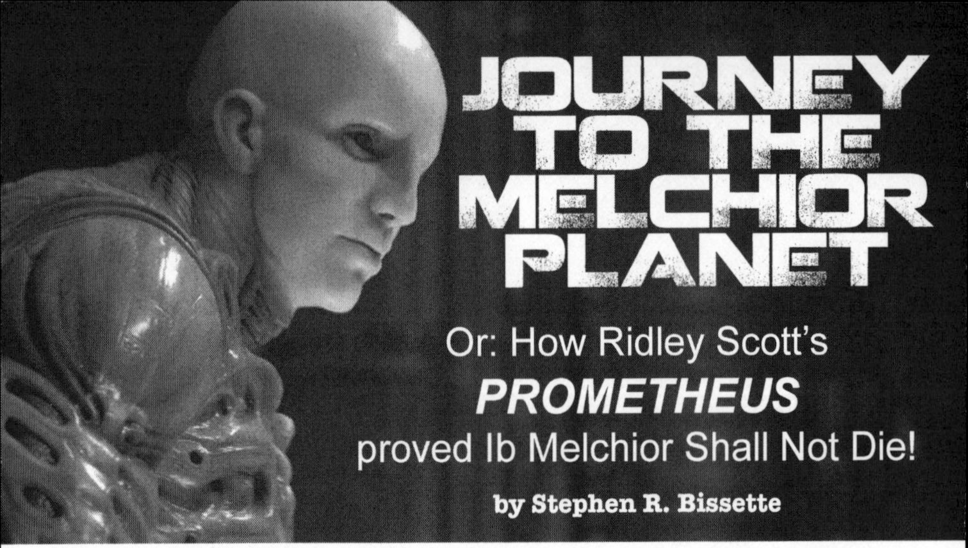

JOURNEY TO THE MELCHIOR PLANET

Or: How Ridley Scott's *PROMETHEUS* proved Ib Melchior Shall Not Die!

by Stephen R. Bissette

Brimming with the mythic, conceptual, and absolutely primal imperative of its title (it's also the name of the ship we spend much of the film aboard), Ridley Scott's **PROMETHEUS** (2012, USA/UK) begins as the ultimate *Metal Hurlant* movie—from the second director on Earth to recognize *Metal Hurlant* as the wellspring for a new vanguard of visual SF (Alejandro Jodorowksy was the first with his uncompleted "DUNE" project).

It's "primal", too, in its story engine: the conceit here is mankind crossing the universe to confront what it believes to be its creator. Or *Creator*.

The first half of the film develops that beautifully, while encompassing the flaws of *Metal Hurlant* (i.e., superficial narrative trumped by the sheer density of mesmerizing, convincing environments and imagery: it is not eclipsed by that density, since that *is* part and parcel of its narrative structure, per all Ridley Scott's films). Like *Metal Hurlant* and its American incarnation *Heavy Metal* (the magazine, not the impoverished animated feature), **PROMETHEUS** also remains fixed conceptually in the thrall of the 1960s, specifically Ib Melchior's **THE ANGRY RED PLANET** (1959, USA) and script for **JOURNEY TO THE SEVENTH PLANET** (1962, USA/Denmark), Arthur C. Clarke's short story "The Sentinel" (written in 1948, published in 1951) and Clarke/Stanley Kubrick's **2001: A SPACE ODYSSEY** (1968, USA/UK)—initially.

But there's much of A.E. Van Vogt, Clifford Simak (specifically his short story "Junkyard"), and Dan O'Bannon (the late father of all things **ALIEN**) here once we get to **PROMETHEUS**' astral destination.

The "invisible-to-99.8% of the audience" visual cues referencing earlier 1960s SF movie precursors to Scott's **ALIEN** (1979, USA/UK)—the fruits of American-International Pictures, a.k.a. AIP—meld perfectly with Scott's visual and narrative tapestry. Thus, along with elements of the two Melchior AIP features I've already cited, we see helmet and costume elements patterned after Curtis Harrington's **QUEEN OF BLOOD** ([1966, USA] to match spectacular footage from the Russian SF films producer Roger Corman had acquired, **NEBO ZOVYOT** [Небо зовет, 1959, D: Mikhail Karzhukov, Aleksandr Kozyr] and **MECHTE NAVSTRECHU** [Мечте навстречу, 1963, D: Mikhail Karzhukov, Otar Koberidze]), as well as costumes and conceptual premise plus "found alien bodies" imagery from Mario Bava and Ib Melchoir's **PLANET OF THE VAMPIRES** (*Terrore nello spazio*, 1965, Italy/Spain), and so on.

The only imagery cues *recognizable* to the average viewer, though, are those the most recent **PROMETHEUS** preview played like trump cards: **ALIEN**—specifically Dan O'Bannon's original concepts—and, above all, H.R. Giger's then-innovative designs for truly *alien* interior bio-tech environments. Presuming all 1979 artistic partners with Scott—Giger, Ron Cobb, the late, great Jean "Mœbius" Giraud (1938-2012)—were paid as work-for-hire creative collaborators, it's also no surprise **PROMETHEUS** embraces, conflates and synthesizes their original (and then-innovative) visual contributions as well. The result is even more intoxicating, given the grander budget and almost-infinite CGI palettes, making this the greatest of all *Metal Hurlant* cinematic successors (I'd argue Luc Besson's **THE FIFTH ELEMENT** [*Le cinquième* élément, 1997, France], as the other).

The human faces front-and-center that dominate are those of Noomi Rapace and Michael Fassbender: the former plays one of those multi-discipline archeologist-biologist-doctors so unique to pulp SF and contemporary SF cinema. She is able to both uncover remarkable prehistoric cave paintings hidden in the Isle of Skye *and* perform startling surgeries (including an abortion). The latter—no spoiler, since the movie tips its hand instantly—is the patented **ALIEN** android character, blonde, engaging, and an oddly vain devotee of David Lean's **LAWRENCE OF ARABIA** (1962, UK) to the point of affecting Peter O'Toole's look, manner, and speech patterns. Rapace—indelibly the movie face of ultimate survivor Lisbeth Salander in the Swedish/Danish film adaptations of Stieg Larsson's *Girl with the Dragon Tattoo / Män som hatar kvinnor* trilogy—is above all the human face of **PROMETHEUS**, and as such also the successor (and, chronologically, given the narrative weight of this film, the predecessor) to Sigourney Weaver's put-upon Ripley character. One could argue Charlize Theron (as the mission's ice-queen commander) bridges the human and android realms, so perfect are her features and composure, central to both Scott's textural/imagery weave and writers Jon Spaihts' and Damon Lindelof's tale.

At a key point, though, Scott, Spaihts, and Lindelof (for all Scott's public statements to the contrary) becomes *so* self-referential not only to **ALIEN**, but to all that **ALIEN** spawned in the 1980s, that **PROMETHEUS** mutates from the ultimate *Metal Hurlant* movie to the ultimate Roger Corman **ALIEN** progeny.

Again, no plot spoilers from me—and I admit my glee with the whole experience exploded as the movie spilled into overdrive—but for all the po-faced seriousness and absolute solemnity of presentation, **PROMETHEUS** becomes a 1980s New World Pictures/Roger Corman movie writ large. Think **HUMANOIDS FROM THE DEEP** (1980), **GALAXY OF TERROR** (1981), **ANDROID** (1982), and especially Tim Curnen's and Allan Holzman's **MUTANT** a.k.a. **FORBIDDEN WORLD** (1982, all USA), meshed with gruesome glimmers of Norman J. Warren's and the late Rich-

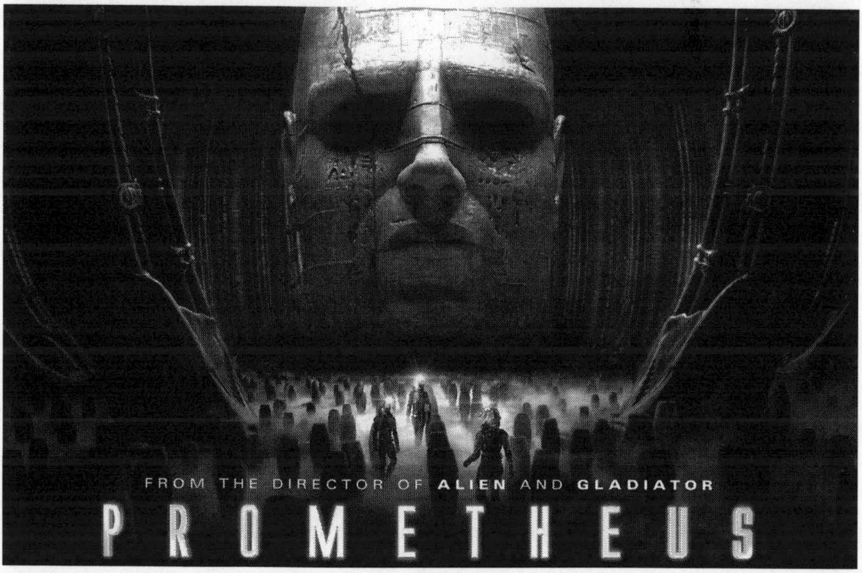

ard Gordon's **INSEMINOID** (a.k.a. **HORROR PLANET**, 1981, UK) and William Malone's **CREATURE** (a.k.a. **TITAN FIND**, 1985, USA [see *Monster!* #15, p. 39]). Then, add spasms and shards of more upscale 1990s-to-present offspring (i.e., franchise co-producer Walter Hill's disowned/orphaned **SUPERNOVA** [2000, USA/ Switzerland], Danny Boyle's **SUNSHINE** [2007, UK/USA], etc.).

Once two of the exploratory party get lost in the cavernous artifact interior, we're back to the *"Oh, come ON!"* turf of Brett (Harry Dean Stanton) looking for the cat in **ALIEN**—smart filmmaker Ridley Scott slumming or presuming *we'll* slum as necessary—so, if you can roll with *that*, as I did, a new kind of fun kicks in. And once the puddle "penisaurus" (as evocative of **FLESH GORDON** [1974, USA, Ds: Michael Benveniste, Howard Ziehm] as it is the thing in the trash compactor in **STAR WARS** [1977, US, D: George Lucas]) rears its fleshy erectile head, the extraterrestrial bioshit hits the fan (*Monster!* readers, rejoice!).

The problem is, the extraterrestrial biology of **PROMETHEUS** confuses and defuses rather than *intensifies* its focus: confronting what is essentially God, in a manner of speaking, it starts getting a little fuzzy once the critters proliferate. It's almost as if the spider-pit sequence in **KING KONG** (1933, USA) took over: hell, not heaven, may be the operative metaphor here. Again, Melchior's **THE ANGRY RED PLANET** and **JOURNEY TO THE SEVENTH PLANET** come immediately to mind. **ALIEN** derived its cruel narrative focus from the biological metamorphosis of a *single* creature: thus, the "haunted house in space" archetype became something richer, more engaging, as **ALIEN** became more than an SF *Ten Little Indians* variant to tease out the life cycle of its creature, and how that was dependent upon human hosts. It was and remains a model of its kind.

James Cameron's **ALIENS** (1986, USA/UK) cleverly expanded upon—even as it occasionally contradicted—that conceit, fusing the ruthless efficiencies of its war movie kinetics and narrative template with the broader (then-new) expansion of its Alien life cycle from singular, essentially

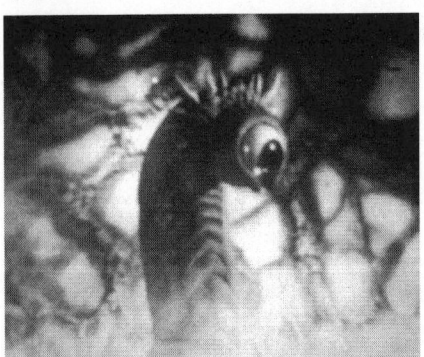

Top: One of the "Engineers" of **PROMETHEUS** (2012), played by Ian Whyte and Daniel James in CGI-enhanced prosthetics designed by creature designer Carlos Haunte. **Bottom:** The stop-motion animated Penisaurus from **FLESH GORDON** (1974), designed by George Barr, sculpted by Laine Liska. **Page 73, From Top to Bottom:** One of Nick Maley's alien creatures from Norman J. Warren's, Richard Gordon's and Nick & Gloria Maley's **INSEMINOID** (a.k.a. **HORROR PLANET**, 1981); two of the **ALIEN**-inspired creatures of **PROMETHEUS**, designed by Carlos Haunte, Neal Scanlon, and Conor O'Sullivan; one of the many extraterrestrial fear-materializations of Bruce D. Clark/Roger Corman/Marc Siegle's **GALAXY OF TERROR** (1981)

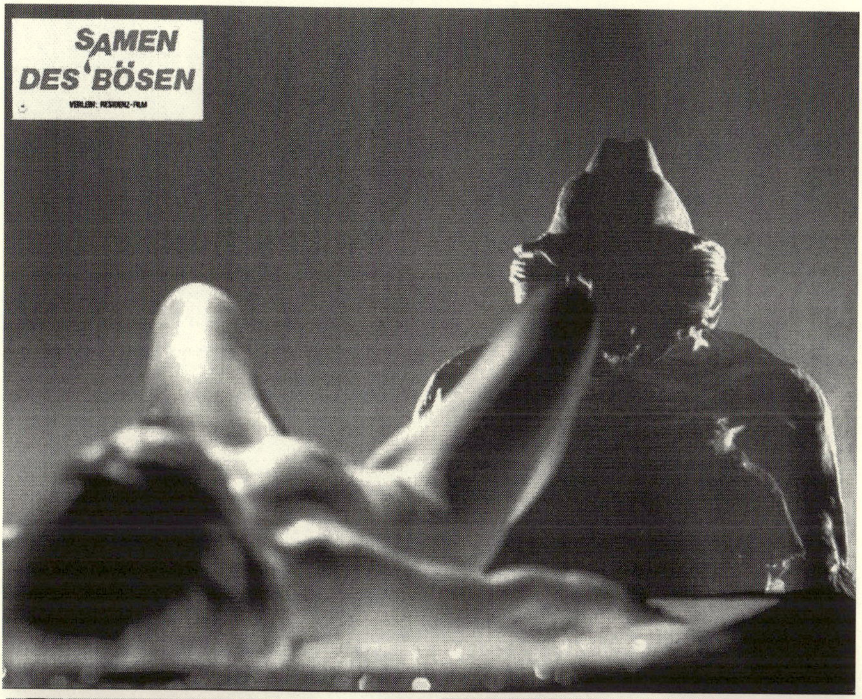
SAMEN
DES BÖSEN

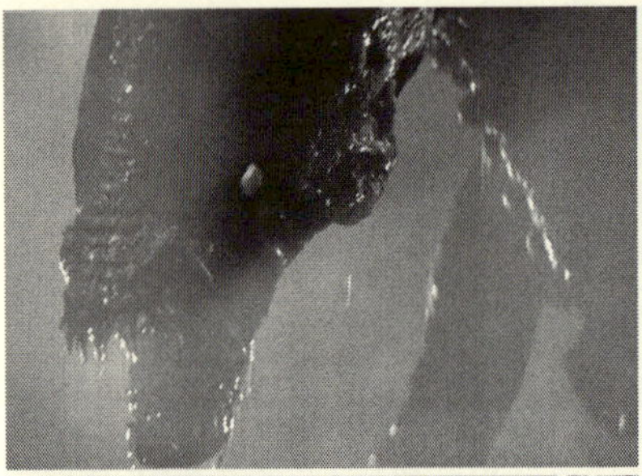

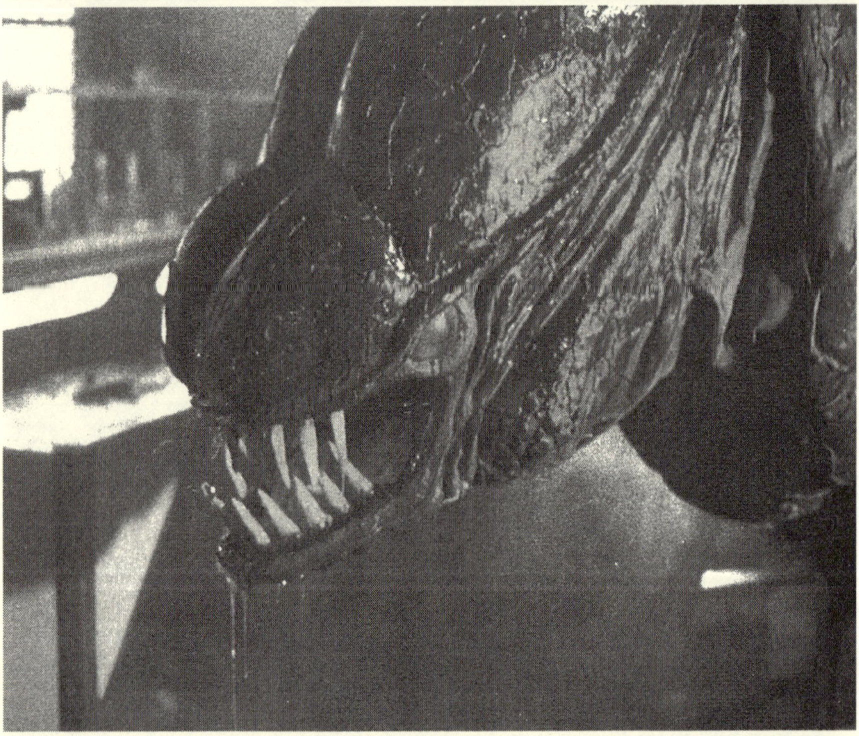

Top Left: Michael McCracken's and Doug Beswick's titular monster from William Malone's **CREATURE** (a.k.a. **TITAN FIND**, 1985). **Center:** the mysterious Martian of Ib Melchior's and Sidney Pink's **THE ANGRY RED PLANET** (1959). **Top Right:** Carlo Rambaldi created Isabelle Adjani's tentacled lover for Andrzej Żuławski's **POSSESSION** (1981). **Above:** The very **ALIEN**-like final form of "Subject 20" in Allan Holzman's and Tim Curnen's **FORBIDDEN WORLD** (a.k.a. **MUTANT**, 1982)

Behind the scenes: Ian Whyte as the Engineer, unknown crew, Michael Fassbender as David, and director Ridley Scott

asexual entity self-replicating via human hosts to the intricacies and wonder of hive activity: with that majestic Queen its perfect fusion of narrative, emotional, and entomological logic.

That was brilliant storytelling and pop cinema.

Once the lifeforms emerge in **PROMETHEUS**, there no longer any singular focal point, nor any real cumulative goal. The creatures, while evocative (and teasing: the audience is waiting for the film to tip its hand—is *this* the proto-Alien? is *that*?) are part of the film's weave, but they're not essential to either its conceptual springboard or its point.

As the infectious/invasive lifeforms proliferate, much like Chris Claremont's messiest 1981-83 *Uncanny X-Men* run (coincidentally, the **ALIEN**-inspired "Brood" thread), they clutter rather than focus the film.

The barrage never lets up, even as Scott, Spaihts, and Lindelof circle, then showcase, repeatedly, fresh and not-so-fresh permutations of other strangely iconic franchise reference points: the "living severed head" imagery (centralized in the **ALIEN** mythos by the unforgettable final dialogue with Ian Holm's Ash), exoskeletal confusions of interior/exterior of humanoid forms (central to original **ALIEN** collaborator Giger's entire aesthetic and body of work), and so on.

Were they running out of ideas, or struggling with *too many* ideas?

But, truth to tell, in the end, *images*, not ideas, are Ridley Scott's meat, and **PROMETHEUS** embodies that artistic conflict. As such, **PROMETHEUS** is a feast, for those with the appropriate appetites. This will either intoxicate (as it did me—hey, I roll with the punches: fun is where you find it!) or infuriate, depending on your disposition. (See my article on **CREATURE** [2011, USA] in *M!* #2 [p.25] for more on this matter.)

Since, as Corman stated at the time, movies like **JAWS** (1975, USA) and **ALIEN** essentially cribbed and co-opted *everything* from past exploitation movies and threw millions of dollars at the screen, I have to say that my living long enough to see it all come full-circle within the Ridley Scott filmography is a source of *delight*, not despair, for this lifelong SF/monster movie junkie.

That said, for all the pomp and swagger, Scott, Spaihts, and Lindelof really don't wander too far from Dan O'Bannon's original **ALIEN** wellspring, or Scott's 1979 execution of O'Bannon/Walter Hill/David Giler's **ALIEN** terrain. The transgressive-in-1979 / *de rigueur*-by-1986 alien/human "tentacle-fellatio" invasive species horrors, for instance, are *still* the main attraction once the lifeforms flourish (and essentially homophobic, as if the worst thing imaginable was still, essentially, a cock in the mouth—granted, that of another species, but that argument is after all central to the homophobia rampant in much of America today, meaning **PROMETHEUS** is perfectly attuned to the 2012-2015 American *vox populi*). Said tentacles-to-mouths are now *fleshier* than ever (thanks to bountiful contemporary CGI effects capabilities), and the cephalopod-fixated fecundity/birthing imagery is far closer to Carlo Rambaldi's creations for Andrzej Zulawski's **POSSESSION** (1981, France/West Germany, see *Weng's Chop* #3) than anything Giger conceived.

Another debt to O'Bannon and Mœbius comes late in the game, with a vivid tableau right out of O'Bannon's/Mœbius' *Metal Hurlant/Heavy Metal* classic "The Long Tomorrow" (1975)—it's fleeting, but by God, it's *there*. That image/panel was clearly burned into Ridley Scott's brain decades ago.

All this clutter (and it *is* clutter, I admit) *feeds* my own orientation to pop culture, and to movies like **PROMETHEUS**.

I had a *great* time with it, beginning to end, but that entertainment was as informed by the whole crazy-quilt confection, and my own lifelong connections to all that was splattered across the screen, from the headier adult aspects to the *"WTF???"* AIP/New World Pictures drive-in excesses.

Approach with caution—in deference to not ruining the film for y'all, I've left out any *hint* of **PROMETHEUS**' most extravagant and outrageous set-pieces, believe me, and per usual, the less you know going in, the more fun you'll have—but it's almost impossible to approach **PROMETHEUS** without expectations. Mine, which I kept at bay as long as possible, were happily fulfilled, but *not* as expected (if you know what I mean; and there is a difference). I was punch-drunk and somewhat giddy rather than disappointed by the finale.

I'll be going back to revisit the movie every couple of years, if only to revel and wallow in its baser elements.

If nothing else, **PROMETHEUS** demonstrates how long the conceptual and creative shadow of the late great Ib Melchior really does stretch—and with news of a **PROMETHEUS** sequel (set on Earth) circulating in 2015, I'd argue we're a long way off from seeing the end of Melchior's long, sweet shadow.

———

Revised and expanded from my original June 8, 2012 *Myrant* blog review, archived at *http://srbissette.com/?p=14694*

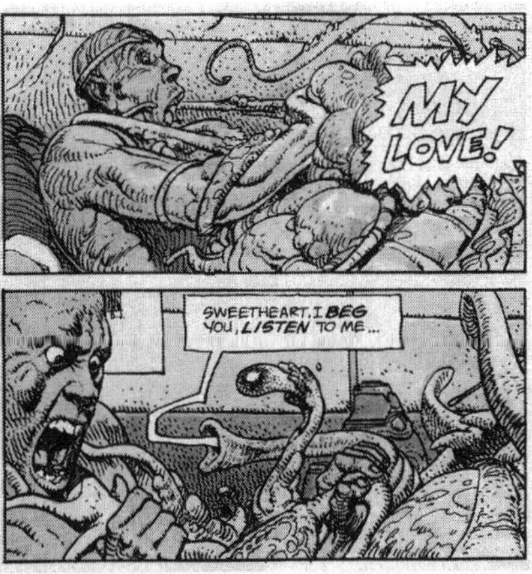

While in Paris in 1975 working on Alejandro Jodorowsky's ill-fated "DUNE" adaptation, writer Dan O'Bannon and famed artist/cartoonist Jean Giraud a.k.a. "Mœbius" filled their idle hours co-creating the seminal and highly influential SF/noir "The Long Tomorrow", which Giraud redrew from O'Bannon's "storyboards" (Giraud's own description of O'Bannon's source material). The completed collaboration debuted (in two parts) in *Métal Hurlant* (#7 and #8, May and July, 1976), first published in English-translated form in *Heavy Metal* (Vol. 1, #4 and Vol. 1, #5, July and August 1977), with a superior translation by Jean-Marc and Randy Lofficier published by Marvel/Epic in *Mœbius 4: The Long Tomorrow and Other Science Fiction Stories* (1987). It's long been acknowledged that "The Long Tomorrow" influenced Ridley Scott's **BLADE RUNNER** (1982), but the unforgettable climactic imagery O'Bannon and Giraud/Mœbius created definitely informed one of the climactic sexualized Engineer/monster confrontations in Ridley Scott's **PROMETHEUS** (2012)

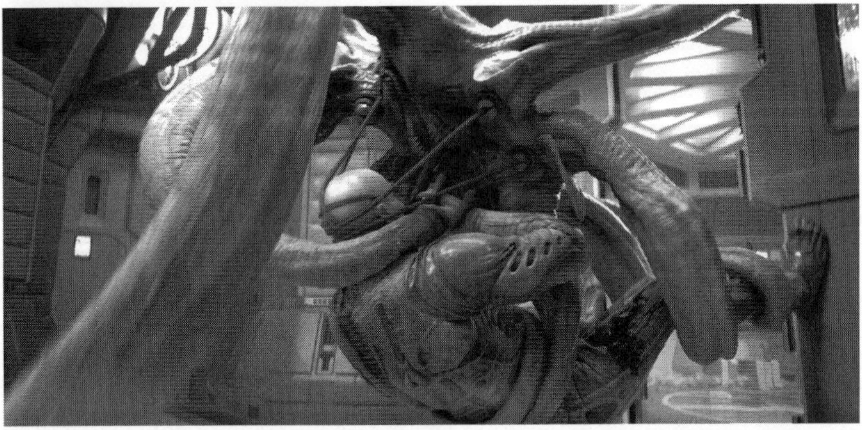

NO WAY THESE ARE LOCAL BOYS!

A LOOK BACK AT 25 YEARS OF *TREMORS*

by Bill Adcock

Finn Carter freaks out as a Graboid erupts from the ground in **TREMORS**. And you'd be freakin' freakin' too!

Horror comedies are a tricky, delicate business all around. With humor and horror being polar opposites of each other, balance must be very deftly preserved; swing too far one way, and it's no longer funny, but too far in the other direction and it's ceased to be scary. Only a handful of films have managed this difficult balance. ***GHOSTBUSTERS*** *(1984, USA) is of course the best of these, but a very close second came out six years later, when Universal released* ***TREMORS*** *(1990, USA).*

Directed by Ron Underwood from a script by Brent Maddock and S.S. Wilson, and starring Kevin Bacon and Fred Ward, ***TREMORS*** *is the story of two down-on-their-luck handymen, Val (Bacon) and Earl (Ward) who wait just one day too long to pull up stakes and leave the tiny town of Perfection, Nevada, for greener pastures. When they do try to leave, they quickly discover that Perfection Valley has become home to a quartet of 30-foot long beaked worm-things, which have begun to prey on the townspeople. It falls to Val and Earl, with the help of the good people of Perfection—all teeming nine of them, at this point—to find a way out of the valley and to exterminate the "Graboids".*

Made for a modest budget of around $11 million, ***TREMORS*** *was a moderate box office success, bringing in $16 million domestically and a total global take of $48 million and change. It spun-off three sequels (with a fourth in post-production as of this writing) and a short-lived though well-loved TV series. Brent Maddock and S.S. Wilson were involved in all three currently-available sequels as well as the TV series, taking on directorial duties as well as screenwriting.*

The sequel features would see new stages added to the lifecycle of the "Graboids", as well as ultimately leaving Val and Earl behind (with Bacon declining to reprise his role after the first film, and Ward after the second) to follow the further adventures of Burt Gummer, a paranoid, anti-government survivalist (Michael Gross, best-known prior to his appearance in ***TREMORS*** *for the TV show* Family Ties *[1982-89, USA]). Burt played strong supporting roles in the first two films in the franchise, before going on to star in the third, fourth and fifth films, as well as the TV series.*

For the purposes of this article, I'm not going to dissect each film individually, but rather look at what makes the series tick as a whole. I'm also not going to delve deeply into the TV series, because I just haven't had the opportunity to sit down and watch it enough to feel confident in discussing it.

French poster

The Writing

Brent Maddock and S.S. Wilson made their feature-film debut with **SHORT CIRCUIT** (1986, USA) and, dissatisfied with the way their screenplay for it was handled, set out to create a film which would allow them a greater degree of creative control, bringing Ron Underwood on as director. Looking to keep costs low, they came up with an idea for subterranean-dwelling monsters—the idea being that creatures which remained underground for the bulk of a film's runtime didn't cost so much money.

Maddock's writing is noted for its strong characters and sharp, witty dialogue, while Wilson writes with a sharp eye for visual effects, having specialized in stop-motion animation. Their combined efforts resulted in a script rife with character-driven humor, in which the quirks and foibles of a small community of admittedly-eccentric individuals—and really, you'd have to be eccentric to be one of the fourteen people living in Perfection—drive the humor, rather than simply having "funny" events befall the characters.

For example, Walter Chang (veteran character actor Victor Wong [1927-2001]) is a money-grubbing cheapskate who always has his eyes open for any possible opportunity to profit. Wong plays the role perfectly straight, without making Walter a clown or a stereotypical money-grubbing cheapskate. Burt Gummer, even more so, could have easily become a cartoonish figure but, again, he's played straight. These characters are odd and eccentric, sure, but they're presented as normal within the context of the film.

Maddock and Wilson not only wrote the first **TREMORS** (1990, USA), they also wrote the three sequels and took over directorial duties; Wilson for **TREMORS 2: AFTERSHOCKS** (1996) and **TREMORS 4: THE LEGEND BEGINS** (2004), and Maddock for **TREMORS 3: BACK TO PERFECTION** (2001, all USA).

This continued involvement by Maddock and Wilson results in a degree of continuity between the films that's rarely seen in sequels. When Kevin Bacon declined to reprise the role of Valentine McKee in **TREMORS 2**, Maddock and Wilson wrote the character out of the script rather than recast the role. 2001's **TREMORS 3** takes place 11 years after **TREMORS** #1, the same interval of time between the production of the two films. The only continuity error I've been able to find in the four films is that the "Welcome to Perfection, Nevada" sign in the first film lists the town's establishment as having occurred in 1904, while the fourth film shows the town being established as "Perfection" in 1889.

This continuity of writing also allowed Maddock and Wilson a surprising degree of freedom to mess with audiences' expectations. They do not allow us to become complacent or comfortable; every time we think we've got a handle on the situation, they throw us a curveball.

A perfect example of this messing with audience expectation comes in **TREMORS 2**, when the second stage of the Graboid lifecycle is introduced. Decades of monster sequels have conditioned audiences to expect bigger and badder monsters, and Earl and Grady (Christopher Gartin) are likewise expecting something significantly bigger than a 30-foot worm when they hear it rooting through a trash can around the corner of a building from where they're standing. They lift their rifles higher and higher in anticipation of facing off against a gargantuan creature...and then a stubby, 3-foot tall "Shrieker" waddles around the corner!

The Characters & The Casting

A script is often only as good as the actors performing it, and the **TREMORS** franchise is filled with great performances and reminders that there are no small roles. Kevin Bacon is an amazingly talented actor, and he threw himself body and soul into the role of slightly-dim-but-good-hearted good ol' boy Valentine McKee. Not only in the delivery of his lines, but in every line of body language, he sells us that he's a lazy knucklehead who finds himself in a situation way over his head and has no choice but to rise to the occasion.

Earl Bassett, portrayed by Fred Ward, becomes an even more interesting character over the course of two films. Initially played by Ward as the smarter of the two, though by no means more motivated, Earl's definitely a cynic right from our first introduction to him, and Ward's seamed, weather-beaten face and gruff attitude speak of a man who's been kicked around by life, and this is never more

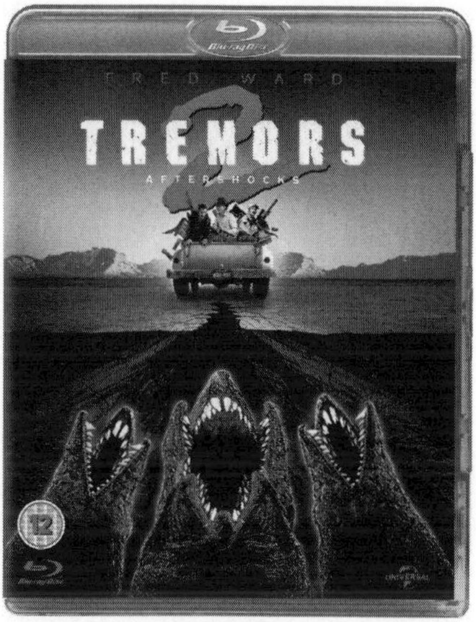

true than our reintroduction to him in **TREMORS 2**. There, he's been kicked around twice as hard, having been screwed out of a variety of royalties for Graboid-related merchandise since the events of the first film, and is now struggling to make ends meet with a floundering ostrich farm. The second film then becomes an arc showing Earl's rise from absolute bottom.

It gets even more interesting when we come to Burt Gummer, played by Michael Gross. Primarily known as the hippy-ish father on the Michael J. Fox sitcom *Family Ties*, the producers were initially very reluctant to cast Gross as Gummer—in much the same way the producers of **GHOSTBUSTERS** were reluctant to cast Sigourney Weav-

A surfaced Graboid in the first film of the *Tremors* franchise

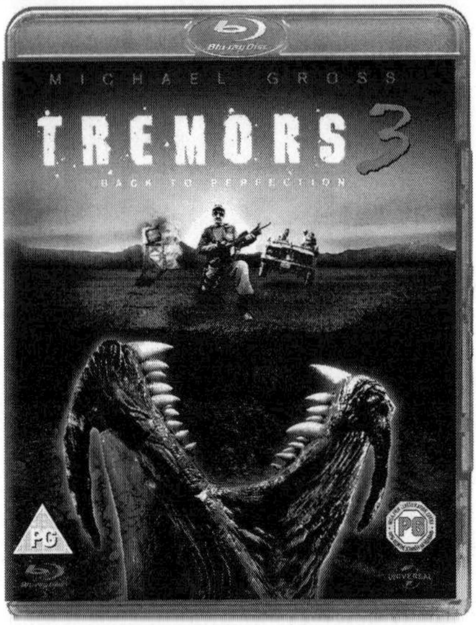

Top & Above: A still from **TREMORS 3** and the film's Blu-ray

er after her performance in **ALIEN** (1979, USA/UK), and with much the same results. In Gross' hands, Gummer begins as a contented individual—he's got his compound, he's got his guns, food for five years, stockpiled water and gasoline, and a good woman, his wife Heather (C&W singer-actress Reba Macintyre) by his side. **TREMORS 2** opens with Gummer having lost almost everything—the Soviet Union has collapsed, the threat of nuclear annihilation is no longer looming, and Heather has left him on the grounds that he doesn't know how to exist without that looming threat. We're literally introduced to Burt in his bathrobe, sprawled in a recliner eating an MRE and staring emptily at a TV in one of the most convincing displays of melancholia I've ever seen in a direct-to-video monster movie. Over the course of the film, Burt experiences what I tend to think of as a midlife crisis: he gets a new ride, he goes on a trip, he fires off a lot of cathartic ammunition. In a way, **TREMORS 2** might as well be subtitled "How Burt Got His Groove Back". **TREMORS 3** finds Burt back at the top of his game, and proving his way of life works when he saves the people of Perfection from a second Graboid infestation.

The prequel **TREMORS 4** takes the story over a hundred years into the past and follows Michael Gross as Hiram Gummer, Burt's great-grandfather. This gives Maddock and Wilson another way to mess with audiences' expectations, as referenced above. We've grown accustomed to sarcastic, paranoid Burt Gummer, and with Michael Gross in the role of Hiram, we're expecting Burt's ancestor to be something of the same, when this could not be further from the truth. Hiram is a stuffed-shirt rich boy from Philadelphia who expects to just be able to throw money at problems and make them go away. Over the course of the film, we get to see him develop into a more Burt-like character, but the sight of Michael Gross in a *Tremors* movie scamming a little kid out of the last piece of gingerbread cake is still a pretty stunning one.

And these are just the primary cast members. There are also some great names among the supporting cast: Finn Carter, Bibi Besch, Ariana Richards, Reba Macintyre, Christopher Gartin, Shawn Christian, Victor Wong, Tony Genaro...*nobody* gives a bad performance in any of these films.

The Worms Themselves

The single greatest key to the success of **TREMORS** as a franchise are the worms themselves. Almost nothing like them appears prior in the history of cinema—though a few obvious antecedents present themselves, such as the Sandworms of David Lynch's **DUNE** (1984, USA) and the briefly-glimpsed monster in Jeffrey Bloom's **BLOOD BEACH** (1980, USA [see *Monster!* #6, p.39]). One thing I find most intriguing about the Graboids is how much of their strange biology is based in real-life science.

The Graboids appear as 30-foot-long worm-like creatures, with thick, leathery hides studded with spines which are used to propel the creatures through loose earth and sand. Their eyeless heads are composed of large, black beaks made up of four blade-like mandibles—one upper and three lower, surrounding a fang-lined gullet and a trio of tentacle-like "tongues", each equipped with a secondary mouth used to grab and grip prey and draw them into the gullet.

The Graboids actually resemble a couple real-world families of worm—their complex bladed jaws resemble those of "Bobbit(t) Worms" (Binomial name: *Eunice aphroditois*), a family of polychaete worms (annelids of the *Polychaeta* class) named after Lorena Bobbitt (*yikes!*)—which are known to occasionally slice their prey completely in half with their scissor-like jaws. The extensible jaw-tongues, and the overall stout proportions of the Graboid, meanwhile, resemble those of "Priapulid" worms (of the phylum *Priapulida*), a now-rare group of worms named for their alleged resemblance to a certain part of the male anatomy.

In documents released by the SyFy Channel, in the form of a faux "Department of the Interior" report on the Graboids, they suggest that the creatures are a highly-specialized form of *Cephalopoda*—making them a land-based cousin to squid and octopi. While the cluster of tentacles surrounding a central beaked mouth makes this seem an apt comparison, I'm not sure I buy it, especially since the "report" seems confused about several key points in cephalopod anatomy (cuttlefish, for example, do not have external shells, despite the report's repeated insistence to the contrary). Even more ridiculous, **TREMORS 3** repeatedly refers to the Graboids as "reptiles"—I guess drawing a connection between the Graboids and actual snakes.

Personally, I prefer to theorize that the Graboids are a side-group of Priapulid worm that somehow adapted to life on dry land. They'd need to develop jawed mouthparts, leathery, water-preserving skin, and be of a large size to fit the Graboid profile, whereas the cephalopod explanation requires them to gain all those, as well as lose their eyes, move their tentacles from around to inside the beak, and develop a whole new method of locomotion, too.

An alternate hypothesis I've considered keeps the Graboids in the mollusk (*Mollusca*) phylum, though moves them from the cephalopod family to the gastropod (*Gastropoda*) family—essentially, making them large slugs that have adapted to dry conditions. We have the leathery skin evolving to protect their moisture-dependant internal structures again, and the beak evolving from the partial shell retained by several species of "semi-slug" that bridge the divide between true slugs and snails. A slug's mouth is the same expansive ring of muscle we see in Graboids, and the Graboid's feeding tentacles could evolve from either the slug's sensory tentacles, which sit on either side of the mouth, or from the radula—a tooth-covered "tongue" used to cut or scrape off bite-sized portions of food before they slide down the gullet.

The slug hypothesis also explains how Graboids can derive enough nutrition to support such a large size and active lifestyle in the arid environments which they inhabit—slugs are generalists, meaning they'll eat just about anything, including plants, fungi, smaller invertebrates; even roadkill can become a feast for slugs. While we mainly observe the Graboid worms being carnivorous, hunting prey including humans, cows, sheep and coyotes, that's just

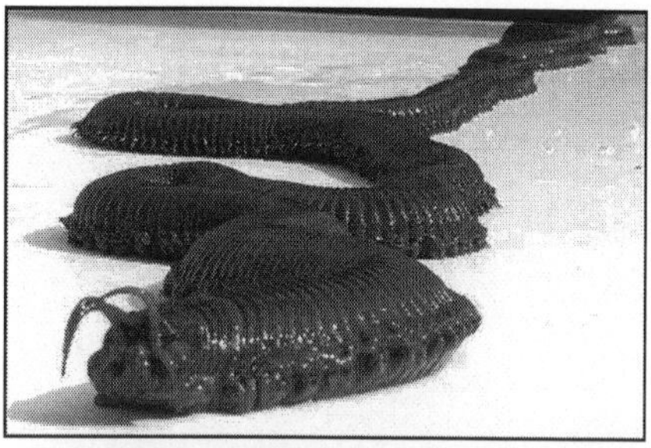

No, it's not a monster millipede, it's a bloody great Bobbit worm comin' at ya!

Yes, They *Do* Bite! An aquatic Bobbit worm, in its ocean habitat

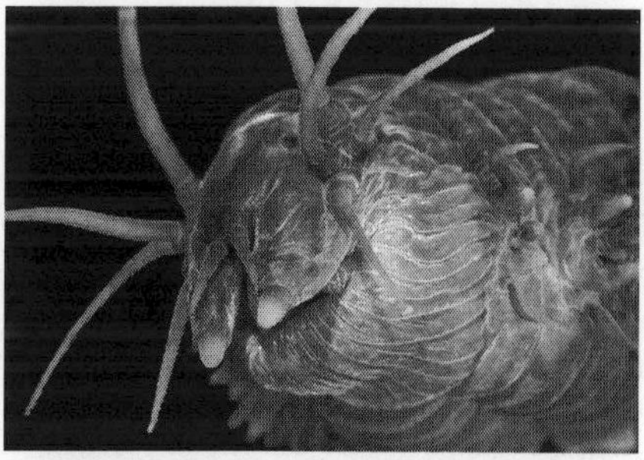

A marine worm of the *Polychaeta* class

A species of sand-burrowing *Priapulida*, in its underwater lair

Hideous Hood Ornament: In **TREMORS 2**, a so-called "Shrieker" dismantles a Volvo

what we see onscreen. If they're sucking down, say, a fungal colony two meters below the ground, we're not seeing that feeding habit. And we do observe that sort of generalist feeding habit in the Graboids' second-stage, with the Shriekers happily devouring any organic matter they can lay tongue to, including gulping down entire bags of rice flour.

Of course, this multistage lifecycle is where the Priapulid and slug hypotheses fall apart. Let's take a look at those…

After an indeterminate period of time (a couple weeks, at least), Graboids "beach" themselves above ground and prepare to give birth. But instead of birthing new worms, they birth a second stage in the life-cycle, known as "Shriekers" for their high-pitched scream. Shriekers stand about three feet in height and between three and four feet in length, trading in their worm-like bodies for a stout, dinosaur-like physique characterized by a pair of muscular legs terminating in three-toed, clawed feet. The quadripartite beak remains present, though smaller and ivory-colored now, balanced against a short, muscular tail. The Shriekers still lack eyes, and have traded in the sensitivity to vibrations that their predecessors used to hunt for an ability to detect the body heat of potential prey.

Most disconcertingly, Shriekers can reproduce themselves at an extremely high rate: once they consume a certain amount of high-yield food—for example, Burt's supply of MREs—they vomit up a mass of flesh that quickly emerges as a smaller Shrieker, which quickly grows to full size, and so on.

After a few days of eating and reproducing, Shriekers shed their skin and emerge as a new stage in the lifecycle, an imago form dubbed "Ass-Blasters". Resembling long, thin Shriekers with three fan-like wings—one down the spine and one on each flank—the Ass-Blasters derive their name from their method of jet-propulsion; two chemical compounds mixed within their bodies and then vented, igniting upon exposure to oxygen, launching the Ass-Blaster high into their air. In the real world, the Bombardier Beetle (of the *Carabidae* family) produces a similar reaction. Though, rather than propel themselves into the air, these beetles use their boiling chemical spray to deter predators.

The Graboids are, as I understand them, self-fertilizing hermaphrodites; at no point do they actually mate to produce young, but instead each Graboid is essentially born pregnant, producing "Shrieker" offspring through a process called endopolygeny (meaning they "bud" new creatures internally, which are genetically identical to the parent organism). Each Graboid produces three to six Shriekers, which chew their way out of the parent. The Shriekers reproduce as much as they can for three days or so, before molting into their imago stage, the Ass-Blasters. The Ass-Blasters carry a number of Graboid eggs inside them, spreading the Graboids as far as they can, thus starting the whole cycle anew.

Other than the Shriekers' "reproduction by regurgitation", everything I've described in Graboid biology exists in nature. This lends a degree of plausibility to the Graboids that many bug-eyed monsters and slime-sucking alien bugaboos simply lack. While the original film famously declined to explain where the Graboids originated, **TREMORS 2** suggested that they evolved on Earth some 600 million years ago during the Precambrian Era. This was later ret-conned by SyFy to the Devonian Period (400 million years ago), because there would have been nothing to feed the Graboids in the Precambrian. Setting their origin in the Devonian has the added perk of making the Graboids contemporaries of the Creature from the Black Lagoon (somebody write that crossover!), which dovetails nicely with the realism of the worms' biology.

The Worm Turns

With the first film having been released in 1990—well before the advent of the cheap CGI that forms the mainstay of modern low-budget creature features—the Graboids have been largely represented through puppetry and animatronics over the course of their career, most impressively in the form of a full-size head that was slammed through the cinderblock wall of the Gummers' rec room. In many sequences in the original film, ¼-scale puppets were utilized, using careful camera angles and matte shots to interact with the cast. From the second film on, CGI began being used to supplement the puppetry, especially in scenes that the smaller budgets of those films could not support practical effects for (such as the shot of a half-dozen Shriekers all climbing atop one another). But even as recently as 2004, with the release of the western prequel **TREMORS 4**, it was a practical effects Graboid that dragged bad guy Billy Drago screaming into its beaked maw.

It's been 25 years since the original **TREMORS** hit theaters, providing an early ray of hope for monster movie aficionados that the new decade would be one in which the monster crawled out from under the shadow of the Slasher, the human monster who had dominated the previous decade of horror. And while the franchise hasn't been as fecund as the masked maniacs have been, there's been a strong emphasis on quality throughout: **TREMORS** films are not churned out just to make a buck, they're lovingly crafted and released into the wild. A quarter-century after the release of the first **TREMORS**, we're now seeing the lead-up to the release of **TREMORS 5: BLOODLINES** (2015, USA), which promises to push the worms deeper into the heart of the 21st Century.

I have my fears, though: this will be the first piece of *Tremors* media not produced by Stampede Entertainment, the production company founded by Maddock and Wilson; neither of these two men are involved in the screenwriting process for **BLOODLINES**, other than it being a rewritten take on their first draft for **TREMORS 2**. According to Maddock, Universal had offered the two the opportunity to serve as executive producers, but, due to being deprived of creative control, they declined the offer. We'll see if **BLOODLINES** is a worthy addition to the **TREMORS** lineage or not once the DVD hits the streets this October. Once I see it, I'll let you know what I think!

NOTE: Information from this article was drawn from the following sources:

The Projection Booth Podcast, Episode 203: *http://projection-booth.blogspot.com/2015/01/episode-203-tremors.html*
Stampede Entertainment: *http://www.stampede-entertainment.com/home.html*
Department of the Interior Graboid Report: *http://tremors.wikia.com/wiki/Department_of_the_Interior_Graboid_Report*

A *MONSTER!* ODE TO IB (Part 2)

Ib Jørgen Melchior

(September 17, 1917 – March 14, 2015)

by Stephen R. Bissette

Ib Melchior left us at age 97—impressive by any measure (and I thought my Mom and Dad had lived long, full lives, passing away last year at ages 93 and 91).

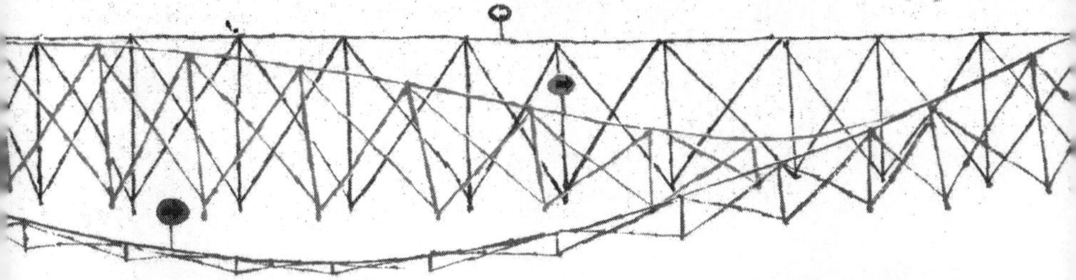

Within his century, Melchior dreamed, schemed, and created much, and would have left an even greater legacy with us, had circumstances, resources, publishers, producers, and studios been able to keep up with Melchior and his heady imagination.

The oldest Ib Melchior artifact in my collection—predating the feature films (on VHS, DVD, and Bluray, including now-rare import editions), *The Outer Limits*, the magazines and the books—is the October 1956 issue of the men's magazine *Escapade*. I treasure it for Melchior's short story "The Racer", reportedly agented to *Escapade* by SF fan extraordinaire, agent, and soon-to-be *Famous Monsters of Filmland* founder/editor Forrest J. Ackerman. "To the crowd, he was a hero; the girl called him 'butcher'..." was the tagline on the title page, accompanied by a blood-spattered painting by Ed Kysar.

"Willie felt the familiar, intoxicating excitement. His mouth was dry; his heart beat faster; all his senses seemed more aware than ever. It was a few minutes before 0800 hours—his time to start..."

Soon after, Melchior scribed, scripted and/or co-wrote (sometimes as the American reworking AIP coproductions overseas) a clutch of exceptional low-budget SF films and television, primary among them **THE ANGRY RED PLANET** (1959, USA [see *Monster!* #3, p.10]), **REPTILICUS, JOURNEY TO THE SEVENTH PLANET** (both 1961, Denmark/USA), **ROBINSON CRUSOE ON MARS, THE TIME TRAVELERS** (both 1964, USA), and **PLANET OF THE VAMPIRES** (*Terrore nello spazio*, 1965, Italy/Spain). A decade later—almost two full decades after its original publication—"The Racer" would become the wellspring for Paul Bartel's savage and satiric **DEATH RACE 2000** (1975, USA). Few have actually read Melchior's source story, so little attention has been given to how much of Melchior's concept actually made it to the screen. Consider, for instance, Melchior's opening paragraphs describing the futuristic vehicle driven by titular racer:

ILLUSTRATED BY ED KYSAR

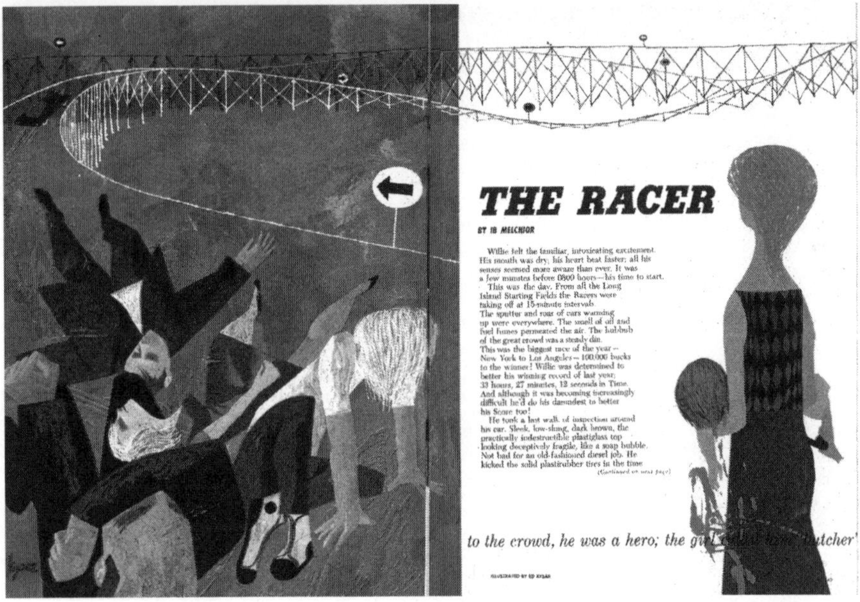

THE RACER

BY IB MELCHIOR

Willie felt the familiar, intoxicating excitement. His mouth was dry; his heart beat faster; all his senses seemed more aware than ever. It was a few minutes before 0800 hours—his time to start.

This was the day. From all the Long Island Starting Fields the Racers were taking off at 15-minute intervals. The sputter and roar of cars warming up were everywhere. The smell of oil and fuel fumes permeated the air. The hubbub of the great crowd was a steady din. This was the biggest race of the year—New York to Los Angeles—100,000 bucks to the winner! Willie was determined to better his winning record of last year; 33 hours, 27 minutes, 12 seconds in Time. And although it was becoming increasingly difficult he'd do his darndest to better his Score too!

He took a last walk of inspection around his car. Sleek, low-slung, dark brown, the practically indestructible plastiglass top looking deceptively fragile, like a soap bubble. Not bad for an old-fashioned diesel job. He kicked the solid plastirubber tires in the time

(Continued on next page)

to the crowd, he was a hero; the

Double-page opening spread from the October 1956 *Escapade*, for the original publication of Ib Melchior's short story "The Racer," illustration by Ed Kysar

"...He took a last walk of inspection around his car. Sleek, low-slung, dark brown, the practically indestructible plastiglass top looking deceptively fragile, like a soap bubble. Not bad for an old-fashioned diesel job. He kicked the solid plastirubber tires in the time-honored fashion of all drivers. Hank was giving a last minute shine to the needle sharp durasteel horns protruding from the front fenders. Willie's car wasn't nick-named 'The Bull' without reason. The front of the car was built like a streamlined bull's head complete with bloodshot, evil looking eyes, iron ring through flaring nostrils—and the horns. Although most of the racing cars were built to look like tigers, or sharks, or eagles, there *were* a few bulls—but Willie's horns were unequalled."

The first kill was claimed a few paragraphs later, and the cross-country race was underway. Rereading the short story today, it's astonishing how fully-fleshed the concept remains.

As with all the films based on Melchior's stories and/or scripts, much is made of what others contributed to make **DEATH RACE 2000** unique.

True, true.

As with all the films based on Melchior's stories and/or scripts, though, Melchior's characteristic imagination is amply present, and in more than "just" the premise.

Speaking about Melchior's *The Outer Limits* second season episode "The Premonition" (January 9, 1965), Ben Brady noted, "Ib, as you know, is a science-fiction freak... He did the most *science fictiony* stories I've ever heard of" (Brady quoted by authors David J. Schow and Jeffrey Frentzen, *The Outer Limits: The Official Companion*, 1986, Ace, p.351).

True enough. In the context of the 1960s, even the most impoverished of Melchior's science-fiction films and television creations were indeed among the most *science fictiony* of them all. Even a first-time producer-turned-director like Sidney Pink couldn't ruin them. They still sang their own secret siren songs, and provided their own delicious flavors, sights, and sounds.

Of the Melchior films cited above, I rank **THE TIME TRAVELERS**, **ROBINSON CRUSOE ON MARS**, **PLANET OF THE VAMPIRES**, and **DEATH RACE 2000** as my personal favorites. Of them, **ROBINSON CRUSOE ON MARS** (helmed by Byron Haskin, script revised and adapted by John C. Higgins) and Bartel's **DEATH RACE 2000** are the two I've revisited most often. Despite **DEATH RACE**'s "Frankenstein" feint (David Carradine's nominal hero isn't what he pretends to be), those two aren't monster movies—but Melchior's monsters must shape this particular eulogy.

It was either Melchior's good or ill luck that brought him and producer Sidney Pink together. Would as many of Melchior's concepts reached the screen, in any form, *sans* Pink? We'll never know. Producer autobiographies are by their very nature an egocentric breed, but Pink's autobiography *So You Want to Make Movies: My Life as an Independent Film Producer* (Pineapple Press, Inc., 1989) was and remains a pip. Melchior scripted and directed **THE ANGRY RED PLANET** with Pink co-producing; Melchior scripted and thought he was also to direct both **REPTILICUS** and **JOURNEY TO THE SEVENTH PLANET**, but Pink decided otherwise. Writing of the misplaced laughter with which audiences regaled the Hollywood premiere of **THE ANGRY RED PLANET**, Pink noted, "As I watched, I became aware of the amateurishness of some of the direction and acting. As I said before, all of these flaws were attributable to me and nobody else, for I had let them stay in the film" (Pink, p.77). Pink seized the helm for his next two projects with Melchior, ironically filming both in Melchior's native country of Denmark; the results were far more amateurish in the eyes of production partners and distributor American-International Pictures (AIP), despite their track record for unleashing "amateurish" product by major studio standards. In his own book *Six Cult Films from the Sixties* (BearManor Media, 2010), Melchior eloquently provided his own account of both productions' post-production (by all accounts, AIP subsequently contracted Melchior to "fix" both films, as best he could, to render them releasable, and he did so with very limited means). I urge the interested *Monster!* reader to read both Melchoir's and Pink's accounts, and draw their own conclusions—preferably after watching the films themselves.

As I noted in last issue's editorial, however, it remains **REPTILICUS** that rules the roost for most monster movie lovers. "I love **REPTILICUS** more," I wrote. "Fun as those films are, they just don't have the allure and timeless wretchedness of the Danish dragon." I wrote at length about **REPTILICUS** in that editorial, and its place in Melchior's legacy: time to move the spotlight. Pink and Melchior indeed collaborated on more compelling and, by traditional terms, more entertaining science-fiction films. Compromised and flawed as they are, both **THE ANGRY RED PLANET** and **JOURNEY TO THE SEVENTH PLANET** are better films than **REPTILICUS** in every way.

If I had to link Melchior's movie monsters with any clear 1950s precursors, it would be the EC science-fiction comics. As derivative of the SF pulps as Melchior's own work was, the EC SF comics—particularly those drawn by editor and frequent writer or co-writer Al Feldstein—share many narrative and visual elements with Melchior's SF films. Some of these are readily identifiable, including the EC Comics adaptation of Ray Bradbury's 1948 *Planet Stories* classic "Mars is Heaven" (in EC's *Weird Science* #18, March/April 1953), but I am thinking too of the *look* of Melchior's movie monsters. The creatures in Melchior's **THE ANGRY RED PLANET** —particularly its lead "Martian"—resemble Al Feldstein's EC SF grotesques more than the work of any

David Carradine was internationally famous enough to propel the success of **DEATH RACE 2000** (1975) around the globe, as evidenced by this Italian promotional artwork (unsigned). **Above:** Ib Melchior had to "fix" Sidney Pink's filming of his **REPTILICUS** script before AIP would unleash the Danish dinosaur on the American public, postponing release of the feature almost two years (Danish debut Feb. 20, 1961; US premiere—in Bismarck, North Dakota!—Jan. 20, 1963). Reynold Brown's iconic AIP poster and ad-art rocketed **REPTILICUS**' allure, promising far, *far* more exciting monster action than Pink's and Bent Barfod's special effects came close to delivering

pulp illustrator or SF comicbook artist I can think of. I note this despite the fact that two vet cartoonists who were Feldstein's immediate contemporaries worked on **THE ANGRY RED PLANET**: co-producer and production designer Norman Maurer, and storyboard artist Alex Toth (hired by Maurer, who worked directly with Toth earlier in the decade as a contributor to Maurer and lifelong pal and 1950s comicbook packager/co-creator Joe Kubert). Maurer and Toth each had their own distinctive styles, and their fingerprints are self-evident to devotees on much of **THE ANGRY RED PLANET**, but I'll be damned if the rat/bat/spider, the goggle-whirlygig-eyed "amoeba", the carnivorous plant, and that three-orbed tentacled Martian don't look like they stepped off a quartet of Feldstein EC SF covers!

There was a cohesive singularity/similarity and an uncanny plasticity to Melchior's SF creations and lifeforms that was unique, even to my untrained eye as a kid. **THE ANGRY RED PLANET** was the first Melchior genre offering, and its menagerie soon populated not only hardtop theater and drive-in movie screens, but countless pages of magazines like *Famous Monsters of Filmland* and its companion title *Spacemen* (after all, agent and editor Forry Ackerman had a vested interest in promoting Melchior's monsters) and their many newsstand imitators. They still pop up as custom garage model kits and in both fan and pro SF and movie monster art, especially the now-iconic rat/bat/spider.

Even more visible in the monster magazines of the era were images from Melchior's next production with Pink, **JOURNEY TO THE SEVENTH PLANET**, which Ib scripted from a Pink story or idea. Pink isn't shy about its value—Pink on **JOURNEY** in his autobiography: "…To my dying day I shall maintain that **JOURNEY** was and is a great sci-fi story…" (p.103)—but it was a derivative work, particularly echoing Bradbury's previously-noted "Mars is Heaven". Note that "Mars is Heaven" had already been

The super-sentient Martian (seen only fleetingly) and the spectacular encounter with the rat/bat/spider in Ib Melchior's **THE ANGRY RED PLANET** (1959) seemed to channel design elements characteristic of artist/writer/co-editor Al Feldstein's distinctive science-fiction monsters for EC Comics in the early 1950s (cover art by Feldstein for *Weird Science-Fantasy Annual* #1 (1952). The tri-eyed Martian mastermind *[top]* especially recalled Feldstein's EC SF extraterrestrials, with their plethora of orbs, mouths, droopy tentacular limbs and antennae, exaggerating already classical (by 1952) tropes of pulp SF BEMs ("bug-eyed monsters")

Another classic Al Feldstein EC comic book cover—*Weird Science* #8 (July 1951), which led off with the story "Seeds of Jupiter" with art by Al Feldstein—and comparative Feldsteinian design of the Martian amoeba from **ANGRY RED PLANET** (1959). Melchior loathed this creature design, with its absurd rotating eye

"borrowed" for a number of SF pulp and comicbook stories in the 1950s and early 1960s. The Bradburyian elements of **JOURNEY TO THE SEVENTH PLANET**'s narrative—in which astronauts land on Uranus only to find the glacial, frozen planet piecemeal transforming into materialized echoes of their own memories, deepest phobias, and (sanitized) desires—also resonated with elements more evocatively and enigmatically articulated in Stanislaw Lem's novel *Solaris* (published in Warsaw, Poland in 1961—Melchior *may* have known of it, but Pink simply could not have, since the first English language translation wasn't published until 1970).[1] Melchior biographer extraordinaire Robert Skotak maintains Melchior had no knowledge of either Bradbury's story or Lem's novel; I have no trouble accepting that, given how in short order we'd seen at least one similar scenario inform *The Twilight Zone,* and, after all, the story Melchior scripted from was Pink's concoction, however simplistic its original form.

Enough on that: more primal, even childish incarnations of the astronauts' fears and desires fuel **JOURNEY TO THE SEVENTH PLANET**. Those desires were embodied by a bevy of European models (all quite lovely, but hardly *sensual*, given Pink's maladroit direction) and smarmily suggestive verbal *bon mots* from lech John Agar, who made it all sound and feel creepy rather than inviting. For me, there was always an appealing claymation quality to the effects when an astronaut's spoken reverie of the home village he's so homesick for materialized behind him in miniature. That sequence in particular had me wondering if Bradbury's "Mars is Heaven" was the inspiration, but the goofy monsters were pure pulp SF, pure EC, and pure AIP. The monsters made the movie essential viewing for a generation of young viewers taking it all in at a suitably impressionable age. After all, it was a monster movie set in outer space that AIP earned such solid boxoffice from with **THE ANGRY RED PLANET**, and that's what AIP wanted *more* of!

How goofy were the monsters? So goofy that even AIP's Sam Arkoff and Jim Nicholson cried "*Uncle!*" and stripped two of the creatures completely from Pink's original Danish edit of the film, contracting with Melchior to replace them with new monsters utilizing minimal funds. Pink's original production and edit featured live-action, full-sized monsters by the **REPTILICUS** "puppetmaster", Danish special effects and stop-motion technician Bent Barfod. Whatever paltry budget AIP afforded the process supplanted one of Barfod's and Pink's crazyhouse critters—a "snake", partially visible in a few published photos (see Robert Skotak's *Ib Melchior: Man of Imagination*, Midnight Marquee Press, 2000, p.141)—with a Project Unlimited furry reptilian cyclops (realized with punchy stop-motion animation by Jim Danforth). The other—a patently-phony taloned, toothy "mole grub" with eyes on stalks, seen in all its *papier mâché*-over-chicken-wire-framework glory in stills which AIP and Pink shamelessly circulated to monster magazines and displayed in theater

1 In a March 18th Facebook conversation about the movie, sparked by *Video Watchdog* co-creator/editor/author Tim Lucas and his online discussions of Melchior's work in the immediate wake of Melchior's death, Nicolas Barbano noted, "It's clear from Ib Melchior's job application letter to the US War Department, reprinted in his autobiography *Case by Case*, that he understood Danish, Swedish, Norwegian, English, German and French, but apparently not Polish." In the same thread, Robert Skotak mentioned that his revised, expanded edition of his excellent, essential 2000 book, *Ib Melchior: Man of Imagination* is nearing completion and will soon see print.

Above: Belgian poster for **JOURNEY TO THE SEVENTH PLANET** (art unsigned), cribbing the key elements (at left) from the AIP American poster art. **Below:** Cover art for Robert Skotak's definitive biography of Melchior, most highly recommended!

lobbies—was replaced by the hairy incarnation of an astronaut's arachnophobia with color-tinted Bert I. Gordon tarantula effects footage from Gordon's black-and-white AIP opus **EARTH VS. THE SPIDER** (1958, USA), gussied-up with a memorably noisy (*glug glug glug*) audience-groan-inducing torrent of gore after the spider is impaled.

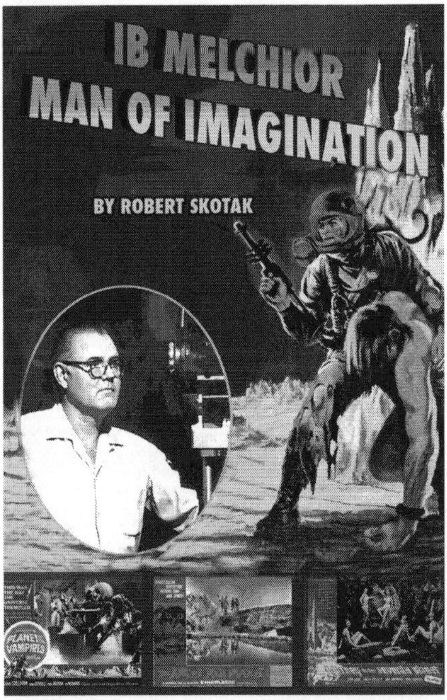

Thanks to laserdisc and DVD, freeze-framing this scene's climax reveals that which nagged at the more perceptive viewer for decades: the giant spider footage hardly meshed with a singular insert shot of a gigantic pincer reaching for one of the astronauts, and it's not the Bert I. Gordon spider but the Barfod bug-eyed miniature pierced by that falling stalactite.

Glug glug glug!

More problematic was the outsized, one-eyed brain—the omniscient intelligence behind the manipulation and materialization of the astronauts' innermost emotions—which Melchior, Project Unlimited, and AIP couldn't so easily dispose of. Shots of the original version's sac-like brain-being remain in the film and populated many often-published official promotional stills, though an attempt was made to enhance the cruder shots with an optically superimposed "trance"-spinning spiral graphic (lifted from AIP/Herman Cohen's HypnoVista prologue to the smash-hit thriller **HORRORS OF THE BLACK MUSEUM** [1959, UK]: they'd recycle it yet again in 1962 for the opening title graphics for Roger Corman's **X: THE MAN WITH THE X-RAY EYES** [1963, USA], and no doubt elsewhere, too). For one fleeting shot, Project Unlimited wrapped a glass eye in a pocket of layered tripe, hardly matching the Danish brain effects (however distracting the optical overlay effects). The entire sequence had a frantic, patchwork lunacy to it; again, this now has fringe benefits. If you look quick and close after the brain says, "...your fears have created the means of your destruction", you can *just barely* glimpse part of the Danish Ben Barfod monster effects creations which were replaced in the American version by one of Project Unlimited's critters.

Sadly, Pink's original Danish-language version seems forever lost, its replaced footage long ago discarded. An "original director's cut" has never surfaced, in any marketplace, in any form (I've asked friends in Denmark to keep eyes peeled for the Danish **JOURNEY** since the mid-1990s. Nada. Perhaps it is indeed a lost film at this point?). Many of the foreign posters incorporated the American AIP ad graphics, suggesting strongly that all international release prints were the AIP edit incorporating the Project Unlimited replacement effects footage.

Danish magazine photo of puppeteer and animator Bent Barfod, whose experience and expertise didn't extend into the realm of live-action special-effects monsters which Sidney Pink engaged Barfod to create for **REPTILICUS** and **JOURNEY TO THE SEVENTH PLANET**. Barfod's monster creations were so unconvincing that AIP's Sam Arkoff and Jim Nicholson insisted upon Melchior's involvement to revise both films for American release

Funny how those stills of the Barfod/Pink production live-action effects were so heavily circulated in monster magazines back in the 1960s; they looked and still look dreadful, but in the extant photos they're perversely appealing creations, like carnival funhouse creatures. Another frequently-published still from the film pictured one of the astronauts lying (apparently) dead, with skeletal legs jutting from his ruptured space suit. This image became a staple of 1960s monster (and humor) magazines (including *Cracked*); it was *everywhere*, including trading card sets (see Leaf's *Monster Laffs* cards from 1967), and it always left me wondering what was cut from the movie we saw. But I never, ever saw in any 1960s

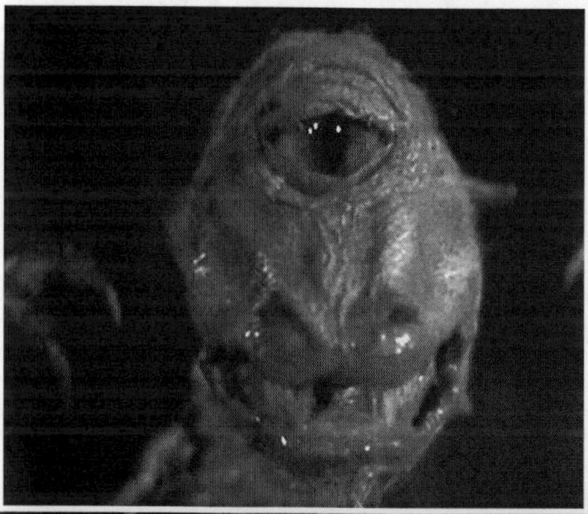

AIP and Ib Melchior's "repairs" to producer/director Sidney Pink's delivered edit of **JOURNEY TO THE SEVENTH PLANET** included this creature. It was only onscreen for fleeting minutes, but AIP deemed Project Unlimited's and Jim Danforth's cyclopean stop-motion animated replacement *[left and below, right]* superior and preferable to Bent Barfod's original full-sized **REPTILICUS**-like "serpent" (partially visible in the still at bottom, left). Robert Skotak promises the first clear look at Barfod's "serpent" in the forthcoming revised edition of his Melchior biography!

monster magazine images of the Project Unlimited cyclopean rat-saurian thingie that Jim Danforth did the animation for. AIP never circulated stills of the beast, to my knowledge or collecting experience.

Per usual for this era and for AIP, the audio elements were a curious patchwork as well: the main theme was a Jack Beaver cue entitled "Spaceways" (from the Chappell music Library), and the extended final credits were accompanied by Otto Brandenberg's bizarre but indelible love theme. I'd *kill* for a soundtrack CD!

JOURNEY TO THE SEVENTH PLANET clearly carried its weight, whatever its flaws, and continued to earn money for AIP and its successors long after its wide 1962 theatrical release. With its lecherous John Agar, its "Enticing 7th Planet Beauties", and mucho monster madness, it remains among my favorite early '60s SF movies.

If there was a sorer spot than Sidney Pink or **REPTILICUS** in Melchior's legacy, it was the unproduced scripts "Space Family Robinson" and "Columbus of the Stars" aka "Starship Explorer." The former spawned, *sans* credit to Melchior, both the Western Publishing/Gold Key comicbook series and Irwin Allen's popular CBS-TV series *Lost in Space* (1965-68, USA); the latter spawned (*sans* credit to Melchior) *Star Trek*. Melchior's ambitious plan to create SF spins on literary classics—"Space Family Robinson", "Treasure Planet", "Gulliver's Space Travels," etc.—was clearly timely and has since been knowingly or unknowingly plundered, pillaged, and pirated by everyone from Irwin Allen to Disney.

Of these, only Melchior's **ROBINSON CRUSOE ON MARS** made it to into theaters. "Space Family Robinson" was appropriated and reshaped into *Lost in Space,* "Columbus of the Stars" into *Star Trek*. Unlike **ROBINSON CRUSOE ON MARS**, *Space Family Robinson* (the comic) and *Lost in Space* and *Star Trek* were filled with monsters, endearing them to me as a kid. My adult qualms with the bum hand Melchior was dealt has only been addressed by Ed Shifres' excellent *Lost in Space: The True Story* (Windsor House, 1996/98) and Melchior's own *Zappp! The Unproduced Screenplay* (BearManor Media, 2011; see *http://www.bearmanormedia.com/zappp-the-unproduced-screenplay-by-ib-melchior*).

Ib Melchior's 1996 foreword to that Shifres book not only legitimizes Shifres' account as definitive—it spells out the *coup de grâce,* in which the initial producer behind the **LOST IN SPACE** theatrical feature (1998, USA), Mark Koch, intended to right the wrongs done to Melchior. Hopes were dashed once attorneys representing the Irwin Allen estate "who were obligated to disclose to the buyer [producer] any and all encumbrances on the property, informed the

WHAT WONDERS AWAIT THESE BRAVE ASTRONAUTS WHEN THEY BREACH THE WALLS OF URANUS?

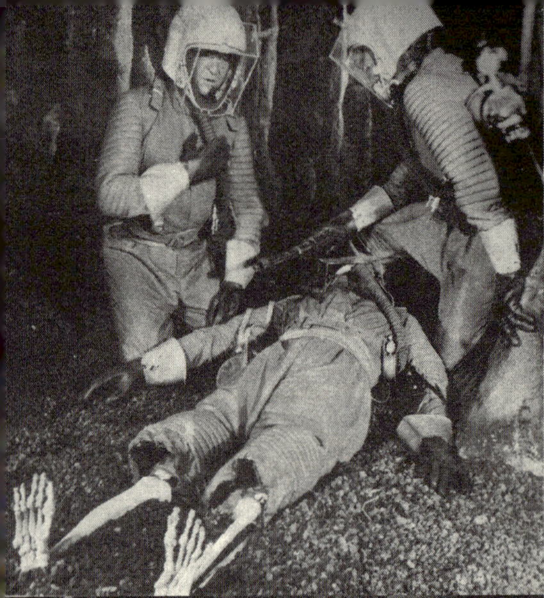

The monsters created, constructed, and puppeteered by Bent Barfod for Sidney Pink's original Danish edit of **JOURNEY TO THE SEVENTH PLANET** appeared in AIP still sets published in magazines like *Spacemen* (Vol. 2, # 2, 1963, from which we scanned these images). However, only a few shots of the Barfod "big brain" remained in the movie AIP released—the rest were cut and replaced. The skeletal-legged dead astronaut was entirely cut; the print in AIP's TV syndication package added to the "brain" sequence a shot from **THE ANGRY RED PLANET** showing Jack Kruschen's body dissolving in the giant amoeba to supplant the cut image of the **SEVENTH PLANET** astronaut being partially absorbed by the brain.

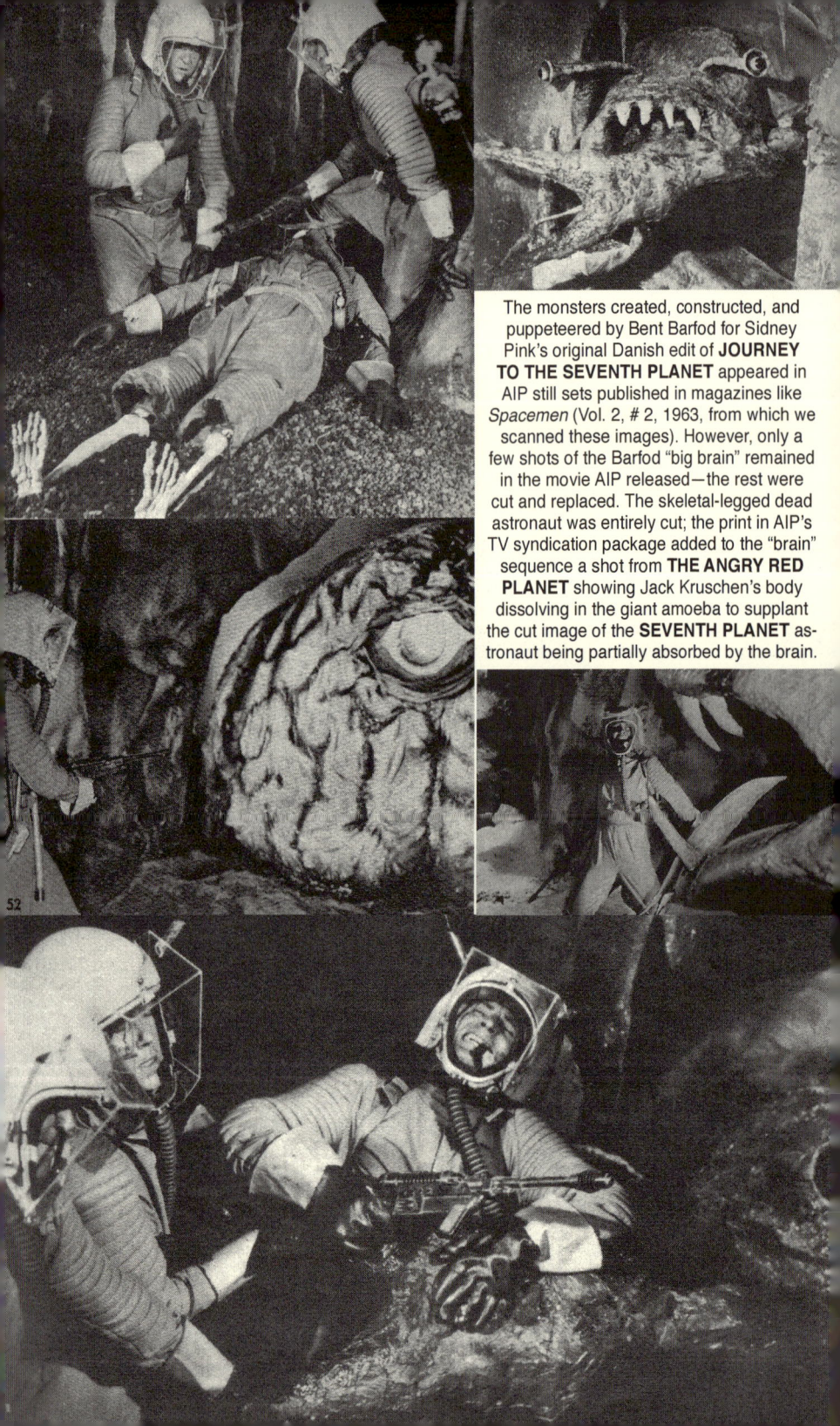

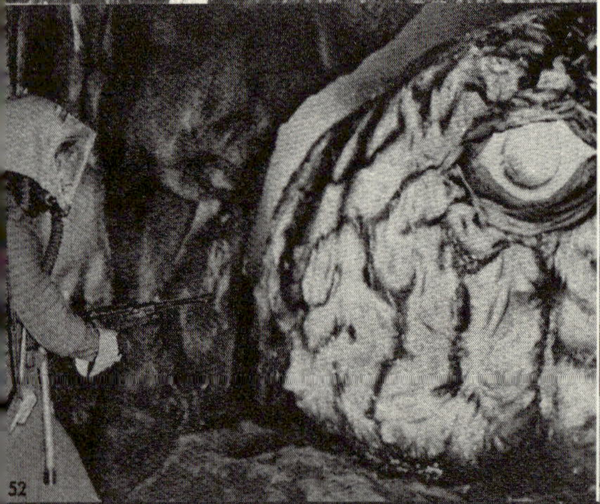

STEP THROUGH THE "TIME PORTAL" ...and you are in the FUTURE before it happens!
SEE: the humanoid robots perpetual slaves to their maker's whim!
SEE: the invasion of the Diviants ...Mindless Mutants of horror!
SEE: women use the Love Machine to allay the male shortage!
APPROUVÉ
APPROVED
THE TIME TRAVELERS
AN AMERICAN INTERNATIONAL PICTURE IN COLOR

Reynold Brown art for AIP's promo, including this title lobby card (note Québec censor's rubber stamp)

Prelude [Pictures] executives that there was an individual, a 'nobody' really, who 'claimed' to have an interest in the property, but the Prelude executives were assured that the claim amounted to nothing," Melchior recalled. "That individual was me." (pp.14-15, 1998 edition). The Prelude Pictures producers found that, as Melchior's own attorney had told him, he "had no case", but morally and ethically believed Melchior deserved some redress. In the end, this meant payment, but no creator credit or byline—Irwin Allen had that locked down, even after death—only a consulting position and credit, and a profit share.

That, too, evaporated when Prelude's contract was bought up and out by its production partner New Line; in the end, New Line paid Melchior a $75,000 production bonus and a flat $15,000 consulting fee, but refused him the contractual 2% of the producers' gross receipts from the film (see "Ib Melchior v. New Line Productions, Inc. [2003], Cal.App.4th" at *http://fsnews.findlaw.com/cases/ca/caapp4th/slip/2003/b153239.html*). Somewhere, Irwin Allen's ghost cruelly laughed; one searches in vain for even a whisper of Melchior's name in movie tie-in books like *Lost in Lost in Space: Pop Culture and Space Adventure with the Robinson Family* by Mark Cotta Vaz (HarperPrism, 1998). Despite having ample room to spotlight a plethora of precursors and precedents (and even dedicate a multiple-page illustrated sidebar to Bob Burns!), and the single mention of **ROBINSON CRUSOE ON MARS** and picture of the Gold Key *Space Family Robinson* comicbook, this and every licensed movie tie-in tome was scrupulously scrubbed of any hint of Melchior's name or role.

Space Family Robinson (Gold Key/Western, 1962-82, 59 issues) was created by writer Del Connell and artist Dan Spiegle; Gaylord Du Bois took over scripting with issue #8. For more on this series, see the Dark Horse Comics reprint volumes (2011+), and *Silver Age: The Second Generation of Comic Artists* by Daniel Herman (2005, Hermes Press)

Thus, Ed Shifres' out-of-print *Lost in Space: The True Story* and Melchior's *Zappp!* remain essential reads.

This leaves us with Ib Melchior's **THE TIME TRAVELERS** as *the* SF feature film most representative of what Melchior could have executed time and time again, had he had a more sympathetic producer and studio. Ever contemptuous, Irwin Allen actually had the balls to rip off Melchior *again*—spinning Melchior's concept into the short-lived ABC-TV series *The Time Tunnel* (1966-67, USA)—but this time, Melchior had completed his production before Allen mounted or sold his imitative pilot, and we can all be thankful he did so.

The film was a two-week wonder. Physically modest in scope, if not scale—ingeniously conceived and filmed as it was, straining at its production restrictions, much of the movie remains claustrophobic and stage-bound—the whole was in its day quite adventurous conceptually. Vilmos Zsigmond's cinematography and the always inventive, in-camera effects lent an invigorating vibe to the film that set and keeps it high and apart from the clunky nature of the Sid Pink collaborations. For once, the production was attuned with Melchior's script, and Melchior proved he was his own best director, as he'd always maintained.

Crude as **THE TIME TRAVELERS** must seem to 21st-Century viewers, the whole was and still is infectiously engaging and—well, *enchanting*. Even the most heavily-dated elements carried and retain their own charm (*Playboy*'s Miss June 1960, Delores Wells, pantomime-playing the Lumichord in a musical interlude with a faux-psychedelic screen "lightshow", etc.), and still beguile. Melchior made the most of every element, including his cast—Preston Foster (of 1932 **DR. X** infamy: *"synthetic flessshhh!"*), John Hoyt, Merry Anders, Dennis Patrick, Steve Franken, Berry Kroeger, and "special person" Peter Strudwick's memorable cameo as "the Deviant."

Unlike Melchior's subsequent visually intoxicating collaboration with AIP and Mario Bava, **PLANET OF THE VAMPIRES** (a film I dearly love, but haven't space or time to properly discuss here), **THE TIME TRAVELERS** has its monsters. Despite the incredible extraterrestrial giants AIP's eye-catching poster and ad art used to sell **PLANET OF THE VAMPIRES**, the only truly monstrous beings onscreen in Bava's iridescent jewel of a movie were the skeletal remains of some long-dead alien crew aboard the ruins of a mysterious vehicle—a shipwreck—whose oversized skulls were extrapolated into the ravenous "vampires" of AIP's promotional department. In all versions of the film, both interna-

The sequence in this AIP lobby card for **PLANET OF THE VAMPIRES** (*Terrore nello spazio*, 1965, Italy/Spain) still resonates, later informing **ALIEN** (1979) and its sequels in oh-so-many ways

Preston Foster and John Hoyt (both at left) oversee the reconstruction of an android in **THE TIME TRAVELERS** (1964)

tional and AIP's domestic US edit, the "monsters" were invisible entities, possessing the dead like the invaders of **PLAN 9 FROM OUTER SPACE, INVISIBLE INVADERS,THE CAPE CANAVERAL MONSTERS**, etc.—a contagion, if you will, rather than the monsters promised by the one-sheet poster in the theater lobby. **THE TIME TRAVELERS** offered more familiar monstrous figures stalking its irradiated future world. Well, they're *sort of* monsters, if you will: Strudwick's pincer-limbed "Deviant," the po-faced androids, the radiation-scarred mutants (these brutes appear to have stepped right off the set of Kurt Neumann's **ROCKETSHIP X-M** [1950, USA]; see *Weng's Chop* #5 [p.169] for my article on that gem). Still, these aren't the Al Feldstein-like beings of **THE ANGRY RED PLANET** and **JOURNEY TO THE SEVENTH PLANET**, nor is the dramaturgy as inadvertently risible as in the earlier Melchior/ Pink films. There's an unexpectedly warm human dimension at play, a cheerful libido at work, and an implicit excitement for and optimism about the future that renders its bloodless but often shocking eruptions of violence (the androids especially suffer onscreen piercing, dismemberment, immolation, etc.) and apocalyptic finale even more chilling

With a fraction of the budget producer George Pal enjoyed for his 1960 adaptation of H.G. Wells' **THE TIME MACHINE** (1960, USA), Melchior concocted one of the first time travel movies to challenge already-codified genre conventions. Melchior embraced experimental film techniques for its unforgettable climax. The plasticity I mentioned earlier as being characteristic of Melchior's movie monsters here became something deeper, more textual than textural. Plasticity was infused into the nature of film itself: the plasticity of cinema as cinema, a more alchemical application, synthesized into the very fabric of the narrative and *the experience of seeing the movie*, of **THE TIME TRAVELERS** itself *being* a movie.

"I did it by taking a four-foot clip of each of about thirty master scenes and running them together," Melchior later explained, "which would be a little less than three seconds per scene, abundantly enough for the audience to recognize the scene and once again experience the entire film, but during an interval of just over a minute. Then I cut this by half—and by half again—and it was still quite possible to recognize then remember the entire scene. I ended up with one frame per scene—the time it would take to blink your eyes—and still the minds of the audience grasped each scene. It was amazing. It worked..." (Melchior, *Six Cult Films from the Sixties*, p.80). This is rudimentary stuff in 2015; Abel Gance had used similar editing techniques as early as 1923 (on **LA ROUE** [France]), and the avant-garde and underground cinema had played with such compressions of time and imagery since the silent era; but this was revelatory in a mainstream genre film in 1964. In this, Melchior anticipated the likes of Stanley Kubrick's and Arthur C. Clarke's **2001: A SPACE ODYSSEY** (1968, USA/UK) and Saul Bass' **PHASE IV** ([1974] especially Bass' original edit, recently restored and exhibited). Groping for subsequent SF movies which **THE TIME TRAVELERS** brings to mind, I think of another a modest-but-ingenious SF gem helmed by another novelist from their own script: Michael Crichton's **WESTWORLD** (1973, USA).

Clearly, Melchior enjoyed his collaborative work with special effects magician David L. Hewitt—and I do mean "magician", in this context, as there's a Georges Méliès-like stage magic audacity to the production. Almost all the effects were shot live, relying on deft illusions, devices, and trickery. Hewitt went on to helm his own films, but never made another movie nearly as interesting (including his "remake" **JOURNEY TO THE CENTER OF TIME** [1967, USA]—one can't consider it a rip- off, since Hewitt co-wrote the original story Melchior improved upon scripting **THE TIME TRAVELERS**). Nothing in Hewitt's later work ever touched the still-effective illusions that Hewitt and Melchior staged for Zsigmond's camera. In a remarkable shot touted in FJA's preview of the movie in *Monster World* #2 (January 1965), *sans* a single cutaway, one of the androgynous androids walks into view, calmly lies down on a table, and has its head removed and replaced. The sense of wonder in such sequences is palpable still, rendering the audacious intensity of the finale's time-wormhole implosion—of the story, of time, of cinema itself—more powerful than it had any right to be.

———

The terminal wormhole caught up with Melchior in this lifetime on Friday, March 13, 2015, just a little over four months after his beloved wife Cleo Baldon had passed away.

Though we are eulogizing Melchior for a small portion of his creative output here in the pages of *Monster!* it must be remembered that Melchior was incredibly creative and prolific—he was a successful novelist, renowned historian, playwright, short-story writer, TV director (in the 1950s), etc.—and son of the great opera tenor Lauritz Melchior. I was hardly alone in seeking Melchior's name on movie ads, posters, and in credits. His fertile imagination outstripped the budgets of every movie that sprang from his typewriter(s), and the one time Melchior had the chops (remember, **THE ANGRY RED PLANET** was his first feature film as a writer/director) and really called the shots—on **THE TIME TRAVELERS**—we were afforded a taste of what might have been on all the other movies based on his springboards, stories, and scripts.

If only circumstances had provided Melchior and audiences such venues again and again. I see his influence in so much of today's media—and wonder, what would he have done with the studio resources slavished on productions like Ridley Scott's **PROMETHEUS** ([2012, USA/UK] a film that seethes with Melchiorian concepts, imagery, and setpieces)?

We shall never know—but I'm betting it would have been a far more coherent and compelling experience, imaginative in ways precious few of the genre cacophonies (whose catering budgets are higher than every film Melchior ever made *combined*) that dominate the summer theatrical schedules ever prove to be.

R.I.P., Ib Melchior!

——

Recommended reading:

Doto, Kip and Melchior, Ib: *Reptilicus: The Screenplay* (self-published, 2000)
Lucas, Tim: *Mario Bava: All the Colors of the Dark* (Video Watchdog, 2007)
Melchior, Ib: *Six Cult Films from the Sixties* (BearManor Media, 2010)
Melchior, Ib: *Zappp! The Unproduced Screenplay* (BearManor Media, 2011)
Pink, Sidney: *So You Want to Make Movies: My Life as an Independent Film Producer* (Pineapple Press, Inc., 1989)
Schow, David J. and Frentzen, Jeffrey: *The Outer Limits: The Official Companion* (Ace Science Fiction Books, 1986)
Shifres, Ed: *Lost in Space: The True Story* (Windsor House, 1996/1998)
Skotak, Robert: *Ib Melchior: Man of Imagination* (Midnight Marquee Press, 2000)

Ib Melchior was renowned for his novels, too, many of which reflected his heroic WW2 service. See *http://www.amazon.com/Ib-Melchior/e/B001KJ0BKY* for more information and access to this body of work

MONSTER! #16 MOVIE CHECKLIST

MONSTER! Public Service posting: Title availability of films reviewed or mentioned in this issue of MONSTER!

Information dug up and presented by Steve Fenton, Tim Paxton, and Dennis Capicik

NB. A hearty "Thank You" goes out to Dennis Capicik for contributing (in his own words) the lion's share of the below info this ish. Where applicable, we ye eds' comments have been interspersed as unobtrusively as possible throughout.

ALIEN SIEGE (p.29) – This is currently available through Image Entertainment on DVD in a 1.78:1 widescreen transfer enhanced for 16x9. Extras include audio commentary with the director and some of the principal cast members (albeit conspicuously minus any input from stars Brad Johnson and Carl Weathers).

THE ANGRY RED PLANET (pp.85-89) – First released on DVD in 2001 courtesy of MGM through their popular "Midnite Movies" line, this single-disc release is long out-of-print, but it has since been rereleased (in 2011)—again by MGM—in a somewhat mismatched "Midnite Movies" 4-pack, which also included Mike Hodges' **MORONS FROM OUTER SPACE** (1985, USA), Albert Pyun's **ALIEN FROM L.A.** (1988, USA) and Edgar G. Ulmer's **THE MAN FROM PLANET X** (1951, USA). Then in 2013, Shout! Factory (through Timeless Media Group) released "Sci-Fi Classics: Movies 4 You", yet another quad pack, which once again re-included **THE ANGRY RED PLANET**. For the record, the three other movies in this set included Edgar G. Ulmer's low-budget US SF classics **THE MAN FROM PLANET X** (1951) and **BEYOND THE TIME BARRIER** (1960), both starring '50s cult icon Robert Clarke, and Ib Melchior's **THE TIME TRAVELERS** (1964, USA *[see separate entry below]*). All of the above-mentioned DVDs are presented in the films' original (?) 1.33:1 aspect ratio. For all you VHS collectors, this was made available back in the '80s by Thorn EMI, and later by MGM in 2001. Lastly, this also appeared on laserdisc in the '90s from Image Entertainment, paired-up with Sidney W. Pink's **JOURNEY TO THE SEVENTH PLANET** (1962, USA/Denmark *[see separate entry below]*).

AVENTURA AL CENTRO DE LA TIERRA (p.6) – At a 1.33:1 ("full-frame") aspect ratio—the standard theatrical format for most vintage Mexican movies—it was put out on Hispanic US DVD in 2004 (now OOP?) by Xenon Pictures (*xenonpictures.com*) without any English, and the copy we reviewed herein was fan-subbed by someone calling themselves Spinal (*muchas gracias, amigo*!). Evidently merely the result of an awkward translation, "Women no longer go down" amounts to one

MGM's US DVD edition

of the more amusing subtitles—if you happen to have a dirty mind, that is (which we most certainly do not [*wink*]). Elsewhere, one character's sub exclaims, "The *moster*!" [*sic*]; to which another character says in fitting response, "What are you saying?" But for the most part, the subs more than adequately convey the onscreen action, and are a real boon to those unilingual types (us included!) who had only ever previously viewed the film in its original Spanish. **AACDLT** was formerly available *en español* on American videotape, and I (i.e., SF) rented it from a Hispanic video outlet called Casa Musical in Toronto back in about 1989. My first viewing of the film was a momentous occasion indeed, and it's stuck with me ever since. As of this writing, copies of Xenon's disc from earlier this millennium were up for grabs on Amazon; just remember that it comes without any English, for those who happen to need it.

THE BLACK HOLE [2006] (p.33) – Ad-line: *"A High-Voltage Sci-Fi Action Thrill Ride!"* Currently available through Echo Bridge Entertainment/ Nu Image, said disc—which includes only mini-

'80s US VHS box

mal extras—is still available for purchase on Amazon at the starting price of $9.59 (brand new), or it can alternately be purchased used for as little as $0.01! (Even if that might well be too much for some people.)

BRAM STOKER'S THE MUMMY (p.56) – DVD cover blurb: *"From Bram Stoker, The Master Of Terror And Suspense, Comes A Modern Day Legend Of The Mummy."* As **LEGEND OF THE MUMMY**, this was released on US video in 1998 on both DVD and VHS courtesy of Simitar and A-Pix Entertainment, respectively, it later appeared on DVD in 2003 thanks to Ardustry Home Entertainment. It is also available as an Amazon Instant Video (solely in SD) as a $3.99 rental or $5.99 purchase. In the UK (PAL Region 2), it also showed up via both In2Film and Metrodome sometime in 2008.

BREEDERS (p.30) – At one point, a number of these direct-to-video, Charles Band-produced (via his self-owned Wizard Video imprint) cheapies—including Tim Kincaid's other direct-to-video film **ROBOT HOLOCAUST** (1986, USA)—somehow ended up in the MGM vaults, but **BREEDERS** was one of the only titles to get an official DVD release back in the mid-2000s (it was also released on MGM VHS back in 1998). Despite the pitifully low budget, MGM's DVD actually looks pretty darn good in 16x9 widescreen. Although technically out-of-print, sealed copies of this DVD are still readily available on Amazon for as low as $2.50, while used ones turn up for under a buck! Back in 1986, **BREEDERS** was originally released by Wizard/Lightning Video in one of those colorfully gaudy oversized "big" boxes (spine #82, for those who care about such details!); thus, for that reason alone, it probably commands a much higher price on the collector's market nowadays. It was also released on VHS in the UK by Entertainment in Video and in Japan on Pack-In Video. Under the present Anglo title, if alternately titled under the translation **REPRODUCTORAS** in the fine print, *circa* the late '80s it was put out on (bootleg?) Argentine PAL VHS by Radicom Video (RDC), with English dialogue and Spanish subs (complete with the titillating cover come-on, *"La invasión sexual"*; a literal translation of the same one used on Wizard's packaging. RDC's came with the exact same cover art). The cheap British "unofficial remake" of the same title from 1997 directed by Paul Matthews (ad-line: *"It's Time To Prey"*) is available on domestic DVD from Ardustry Home Entertainment.

THE CURSE OF THE WEREWOLF (p.65) – Released in the US in 2005 as part of "The Franchise Collection: The Hammer Horror Series", this 2-disc set includes 8 films spread over two double-sided discs (a pair per side), and although many of the earlier pressings had the tendency to freeze and/or pixelate at certain sections, this has since been fixed in later pressings. If you want to test your discs, simply scan through them, and if they freeze at any point, your discs are unfortunately defective. Other films housed in this attractively packaged set include Terence Fisher's **THE BRIDES OF DRACULA** (1960) and **THE PHANTOM OF THE OPERA** (1962); Freddie Francis' **PARANOIAC!** and **NIGHTMARE** (both 1963), plus **THE EVIL OF FRANKENSTEIN** (1964 [see *Monster!* #13, pp.3 & 17]), Don Sharp's **THE KISS OF THE VAMPIRE** (a.k.a. in altered form as **KISS OF EVIL**, 1963) and Peter Graham Scott's **NIGHT CREATURES** (a.k.a. **CAPTAIN CLEGG**, 1962, all UK). Fans of this film with multi-region players have access to a number of great overseas editions, including a fantastic German Blu-ray (under the title **DER FLUCH VON SINIESTRO**) from Anolis Entertainment, which contains numerous documentaries and a commentary track (in German only, though). In the UK, Final Cut Entertainment released a 2-disc "Special Edition" steelbook with similar extras as the German Blu-ray; they also released a standard single-disc edition as well. In Spain, Feel Films also released it on Blu-ray under the title **LA MALDICIÓN DEL HOMBRE LOBO**. **THE CURSE OF THE WEREWOLF** was also a long-time VHS staple in the US and Canada (released by MCA/Universal) getting its first release in 1987, and then once again in 1992.

DONT BE AFRAID OF THE DARK (p.27) – This first appeared on DVD in the US as part of the Warner Archive Collection in 2008, and then a subsequent "Special Edition"—again from Warner Archive—turned up in 2011 in a much brighter, re-mastered version, with the added bonus of a commentary track with Steve Barton from Dread Central, along with **FINAL DESTINATION** (2000, USA) screenwriter Jeff Reddick and *Fangoria* writer Sean Abley. An earlier DVD issued in Japan by Trash Mountain Video paired it up with Bill L. Norton's awesome TV movie **GARGOYLES** (1972, USA). In 1984, U.S.A. Home Video released **DBAOTD** in one of those big, oversized boxes, boasting the tagline, *"Now You See Them, Now You Don't... Now You Die!"* Co-written/co-produced by Guillermo Del Toro and directed by Troy Nixey, the film was of course remade under the same title in 2010; but that "reboot"—complete with totally different CG critters, natch—is generally held in much lower esteem than the original.

DR. TERROR'S HOUSE OF HORRORS (p.67) – Although it was released in the US on VHS by NTA Home Entertainment way back in 1984, and then again in 1989 courtesy of Republic Pictures (with inferior cover-art), this has yet to turn up on digital disc in North America. It has been available in the UK (as a PAL region 2 disc) since 2003, when Anchor Bay issued it on DVD both as a single disc release and as part of their Amicus Collection in a fancy, coffin-shaped box set, which also included Roy Ward Baker's gothic shocker **--AND NOW THE SCREAMING STARTS!** (1973, UK) and the same director's **ASYLUM** (1972, UK), plus Peter Duffell's **THE HOUSE THAT DRIPPED BLOOD** (1971, UK); both those latter titles are multi-story horror omnibuses. In addition, the set includes Paul Annett's pseudo-Blaxploitation werewolf whodunit **THE BEAST MUST DIE** (1974, UK) and a British documentary short entitled *Inside the Fear Factory* (2003). **DR. TERROR'S HOUSE OF HORRORS** was subsequently released in the UK—again by Anchor Bay—in 2006, and then yet again in 2010, this time by Odeon Entertainment. In Australia, it was released by Umbrella Entertainment in 2005 as part of their "Amicus – The Studio That Dripped Blood" box set, which was identical in content to the earlier UK set (albeit minus the distinctive coffin packaging); except that it only contained a shortened featurette version of *Inside the Fear Factory* and it also contained John Llewellyn Moxey's moody **THE CITY OF THE DEAD** (a.k.a. **HORROR HOTEL**, 1959, USA/UK), which was produced by Milton Subotsky but isn't technically an Amicus production, as it was actually produced for the Vulcan company. In France, **DTHOH** was released by DVDY Films as part of yet another box set ("The Peter Cushing Collection") under the title **LE TRAIN DES ÉPOUVANTES**, which also included Vernon Sewell's lesser-seen **THE BLOOD BEAST TERROR** (a.k.a. **THE VAMPIRE-BEAST CRAVES BLOOD**, 1968), Terence Fisher's **ISLAND OF TERROR** (1966) and Freddie Francis' **THE CREEPING FLESH** (1973, all UK). Lastly, it was released in both Italy by Pulp Video as **LE CINQUE CHIAVI DEL TERRORE** and in Germany by Koch Media **DIE TODESKARTEN DES DR. SCHRECK**.

EVIL IN THE WOODS (p.34) – As with Massacre Video's earlier Cinevest acquisition **THE NOSTRIL PICKER** (1987, USA), the present title—newly released in 2015—was originally picked-up as part of a larger package of films by Vinegar Syndrome. In spite of its low-budget origins, Massacre Video does a solid job of bringing this to DVD in a decent transfer, and, although unspectacular, it is much better than any previous VHS release of **EITW**. Extras include a DVD-ROM of the film's dialogue, and, just like the film itself, this is a hilariously jumbled mess; there is also a small but welcome stills gallery (including some rare scans of the film's VHS releases), plus trailers for some of Massacre Video's current and upcoming releases, including Adam Ahlbrandt's **THE CEMETERY** (2013, USA), Nick Palumbo's **NUTBAG** (2000, USA) and Michel Ricaud's **SEXANDROIDE** (1987, France). Back in the

Massacre Video's brand-new DVD edition

Don't be taken in by this bogus fan-made Blu-ray cover; it's as fake as a sideshow mermaid!

'80s, **EITW** was available on VHS in Australia on Palace Explosive, in Japan on King Video and in Puerto Rico/USA on "grey market" tape from New Video Entertainment.

GIGANTES PLANETARIOS (p.15) – A somewhat-too-dark if more than watchable full-length (87½-minute) upload ripped from Mexican TV—in Spanish, sans English, natch—is available for viewing on YouTube at the link entitled "Gigantes Planetarios (Alfredo B. Crevenna 1965) (TvRip)" (*https://www.youtube.com/watch?v=SnxVrdxRS-fI*). Forget the way crappier version at the link called "Gigantes planetarios peliculas en español completas 2014", because not only is it much fuzzier, but the runtime is way overlong (2+ hours!), leading me to suspect that there must be some interruptions interspersed throughout (I didn't bother checking, that's how shitty it looks). This one really stretches *Monster!*'s stringent criteria for what constitutes a monster movie, because there aren't any actual monsters in it…but there are some goofy-looking humanoid aliens in helmets with rabbit-ear antennae on and lotsa tacky "sci-fi" hardware such as rockets, spacesuits and rayguns, if that's any consolation.

LA ISLA DE LOS DINOSAURIOS (p.16) – In 2009, Navarre Corporation of the US released this on NTSC Region 1 DVD as a single-disc double-bill (*"2 alarmes peliculas!"*) with same director Crevenna's **EL HOMBRE QUE LOGRÓ SER INVISIBLE** ([1958] known in English as both **INVISIBLE MAN IN MEXICO** and **THE NEW INVISIBLE MAN**), but the disc came with Spanish dialogue only, without English subs. Last year sometime, I (SF) found a pretty nice quality upload of the film on YouTube; however, this version seems to have since vanished without a trace, as can sometimes happen at said site (I'm glad I d-loaded it when I had the chance!). However, for a sneak preview of this cut-and-paste patchwork oddity, check out the link called "La Isla de los Dinosaurios (1967) trailer" at YT.

JOURNEY TO THE SEVENTH PLANET (pp.85-94) – Issued on DVD by MGM as part of their "Midnite Movies" collection, this was paired up with Edward L. Cahn's proto zombie flick **INVISIBLE INVADERS** (1959, USA); both films were presented in their original 1.33:1 aspect ratio. In 2011, MGM issued this film as part of a 4 Movies set (again under the "Midnite Movies" moniker) with Michael Laughlin's **STRANGE INVADERS** (1983, USA), Tobe Hooper's **INVADERS FROM MARS** (1986, USA) remake, and, once again, **INVISIBLE INVADERS**.

THE KEEP (p.17) – The film was formerly ('80s/'90s) available on Betamax/VHS cassette from Paramount Home Video, presented in its original theatrical aspect ratio. In Australia, it was once available on VHS/Beta from CIC Video. Due to legal technicalities, this is available to view on Netflix only in the UK and Ireland, but elsewhere it can be either rented (for $2.99) or purchased (for $9.99) as an Amazon instant video, albeit only in the film's greatly-truncated 96m. edit and in the SP mode (Mann's original vision ran around 3 hours in length). Despite a bogus Blu-ray cover we found via Google which wishfully claims to be the "30th Anniversary Special Edition", **THE KEEP** is currently unavailable worldwide on either DVD or Blu; this due to an ongoing copyrights issue involving Virgin Music (who now own the music rights) over ownership of Tangerine Dream's score. And speaking of its score, several bootleg releases have been made available over the years, including one put out by Blue Moon in 1994. Much like the soundtrack, numerous bootleg DVD-Rs of this film have been circulated, so diehard fans wishing to view it in optimal form can only patiently bide their time until a legitimate full-length release transpires…just don't hold your breath!

MONSTERS: DARK CONTINENT (p.21) – Tagline: *"Fear Has Evolved."* The official street date of the US DVD is June 2nd, 2015, but it is currently available as an HD insta-vid download from Amazon for rent ($6.99) or purchase ($14.99). In the UK, the film is available on DVD from Vertigo Films.

PROMETHEUS (p.70) – Available on disc from 20th Century Fox, both in a double-disc Blu-ray set and as a single-disc DVD. This A-list title is available from innumerable sources, so we shan't dwell on them here. Just do an online search, and take your pick of all the options!

PYASI APSARA (p.41) – Released in a VCD set and also as part of a 3-in-1 DVD collection, this was put out in both formats by the prolific Indian company Captain Video (check at *induna.com*). No subtitles are included with either if those versions. The film is also up for viewing on YouTube in at least three different versions: two full-length and one broken up into multiple sections (don't you just *hate* that?!). Complete copies can be found at the links "Pyasi Apsara - Super Hit Romantic Hindi Movie" (*https://www.youtube.com/watch?v=hOV7THAG9I4*) and "Pyasi Apsara - Full Length Hindi Movie" (*https://www.youtube.com/watch?v=rPNSl4LbKQg*). Both have not just one but two Captain Video watermarks loudly plastered on them throughout, but the former of the two YT versions is preferable, as its picture quality is somewhat better. Said version evidently runs about a minute longer than the latter mentioned version, but we're not sure whether it actually contains extra footage or not. But by all means compare the two prints and find out for yourselves! ☺

REPTILICUS (pp.85-92) – Originally released by MGM in 2001 (as part of their popular Midnite Movies line) as a single disc release, this edition was fullscreen and is now long out-of-print. In 2013, Shout! Factory (through Timeless Media Group) released the film as part of their "Movies 4 You: More Sci-Fi Classics" line in the same fullscreen print, along with Edgar G. Ulmer's **THE AMAZING TRANSPARENT MAN** (1960, UK), Ewald André Dupont's **THE NEANDERTHAL MAN** (1953) and Joseph Green's **THE BRAIN THAT WOULDN'T DIE** (1959, both USA). For those with multi-region capabilities, the original Danish version is also available on the Sandrew/Metronome label. The fine folks at Scream Factory have also announced a Double Feature Blu-ray (along with Ovidio G. Assonitis' **TENTACLES** [1977, USA]) to be released on June 16th, 2015.

A double Blu-ray due to be released this June

ROBINSON CRUSOE ON MARS (p.92) – Available as a "Director-Approved Blu-Ray Special Edition" (in its full glorious 2.35:1 aspect ratio) as part of the Criterion Collection. Loaded with extras, this state-of-the-art Criterion edition even includes co-scripter Ib Melchior's "Brief Yargorian Vocabulary", a glossary of the alien (as in Martian) language heard spoken in the film. Melchior also contributes to an audio commentary, as did stars Paul Mantee and Victor Lundin, production designer Al Nozaki, FX tech and Melchior biographer Robert Skotak; extras also include excerpts of a 1979 audio interview with **RCOM**'s director, Byron Haskin. The film's spacy soundtrack, composed by Van Cleave was issued on CD by FSM as part of their "Silver Age Classics" series.

SHE DEVIL (p.46) – Long unavailable, Olive Films finally debuted this on both DVD and Blu-ray in February of 2013 in a beautiful anamorphic widescreen print, which retained the film's original 2.35:1 "Regalscope" aspect ratio; while their print is largely pristine and sharp, Olive's edition comes with neither any supplemental material nor subtitle options. Online links to 3 other dramatizations of

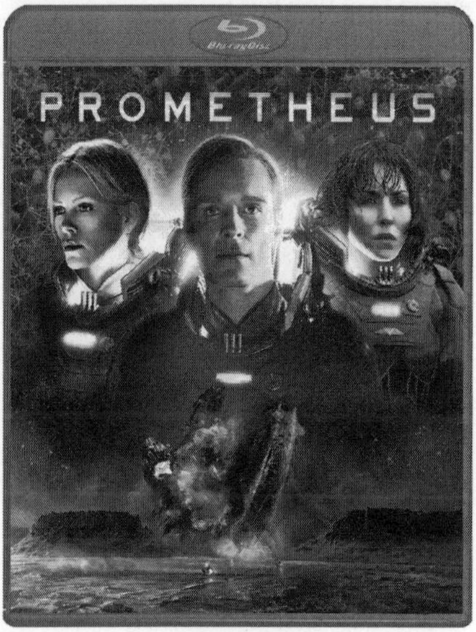

US Blu-ray

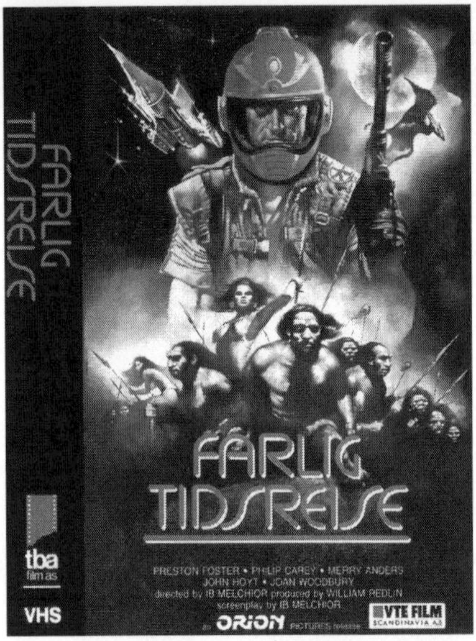

The decidedly fanciful 1980s Norwegian VHS cover for **THE TIME TRAVELERS**

the same story—1 made for radio and 2 made for TV—can be found at the foot of p.54, as well as links to further information about "The Adaptive Ultimate", the Stanley G. Weinbaum SF tale on which all the versions were based. In 2008, Wonder Audio put out an hour-long spoken word version of said story (read by Mark Douglas Nelson) which was made available for streaming at Audible and iTunes.

THE SLIME PEOPLE (p.35) – Made available on Beta/VHS tape by Video Gems back in the '80s, this was later released on domestic DVD by Rhino Video in a no-frills fullscreen edition. More recently in 2013, as the second feature of their "Creepy Creature Double Feature Vol. 2" set, it was issued by VCI Entertainment in a widescreen edition, double-billed with another '60s psychotronic trash classic, Herbert L. Strock's **THE CRAWLING HAND** (1963, USA), which was likewise co-produced by the present film's Joseph F. Robertson, who also filled the same function on Gerd "*The Outer Limits*" Oswald's cheapo "killer bacterium" spy flick **AGENT FOR H.A.R.M.** (1966, USA). Special features included with VCI's release are original theatrical trailers for both films, plus audio interviews with leading lady Susan Hart and film historian Tom Weaver about **THE SLIME PEOPLE**.

Olive Films' US Blu-ray jacket

TALE OF THE MUMMY (p.58) – This first appeared on Japanese DVD courtesy of Beam Entertainment under its original title **TALOS THE MUMMY**, then, a year later, it showed up on US DVD from Dimension/Buena Vista. Both of these early releases retained the original 2.35:1 aspect ratio, but were unfortunately not enhanced for 16x9. It eventually made its way to Blu-ray in 2012 via Echo Bridge Entertainment, and a few months later it showed on up on yet another Blu (from Echo Bridge once again), this time paired-up with Chuck Comisky's **BENEATH LOCH NESS** (2001, USA); both these discs are now out-of-print, but can still be obtained on Amazon for pretty damn cheap. **TOTM** also showed up in France on TFI Video under the title **LE MALÉDICTION DE LA MOMIE**, which likewise retained the original 2.35:1 aspect ratio, with 16x9 enhancement.

THE TIME TRAVELERS (pp.95-98) – Originally released in the '80s on VHS by Thorn EMI/HBO Video, this finally turned up in the digital format in 2013 when Shout! Factory (in conjunction with Timeless Media Group) released it as part of their "Movies 4 You: Sci-Fi Classics" set, which also included Edgar G. Ulmer's **THE MAN FROM PLANET X** and **BEYOND THE TIME BARRIER** (1960, USA) and Ib Melchior's **THE ANGRY RED PLANET** (1960, USA *[see separate entry above]*). Like most of these budget-priced "Movies 4 You" quad packs from Timeless Media Group, the picture quality suffers simply due to the fact that they have all been squished onto one DVD together. **TTT** was formerly (*circa* the '80s) available on Beta/VHS cassette in Norway from TBA Film, in its original English dialogue with Norwegian subtitles.

TREMORS series (pp.77-83) – Currently available through Universal, the entire series (13 episodes) is spread over 3 DVD's. Although quite inexpensive, there have been some grumblings online about the actual presentations, which have been released fullscreen as opposed to their original widescreen (1.85:1) airings on the Sci-Fi Channel.

WEREWOLF OF LONDON (p.62) – First issued on DVD as a "Wolf Man Double Feature" courtesy of Universal, this was paired-up with Jean Yarbrough's lackluster **SHE-WOLF OF LONDON** (1946, USA). It has since been released on numerous collections (all from Universal) including "The Wolf Man: The Legacy Collection", the "Monster Legacy DVD Gift Set" (which also included miniature busts of Dracula, Frankenstein and The Wolf Man), and, most recently, as part of the massive "Universal Classic Monsters Complete 30-film Collection". For you VHS collectors, Universal released this on tape in 1998.

WEREWOLF SHADOW (p.68) – First issued on US DVD by Anchor Bay in 2002 in a nice uncut and anamorphic presentation, which also included an interview with Paul Naschy a.k.a. Jacinto Molina. The same year, this also showed up in its alternate 81-minute US version **THE WEREWOLF VS. THE VAMPIRE WOMAN** in the "Pray for Death" 4-pack from Brentwood Entertainment, which also included Amando de Ossorio's 4th and final *Blind Dead* entry **THE NIGHT OF THE DEATH CULT** (a.k.a. **THE NIGHT OF THE SEAGULLS**, *La noche de las gaviotas*, 1975, Spain), along with Joseph Mazzuca's **SISTERS OF SATAN** (1977, USA) and Alan Gibson's **THE SATANIC RITES OF DRACULA** (1974, UK [see *Monster!* #13, p.35). In 2008, **WS** was released by BCI Eclipse/Deimos, which included both the 91-minute uncut Spanish version and the shorter 81-minute version; it was later rereleased by BCI Eclipse, as a double feature with Carlos Aured's **CURSE OF THE DEVIL** (*El retorno de Walpurgis*, 1973, Spain [see *M!* #8, p.48]). In December 2014, as a Region B-locked Blu-ray, **WEREWOLF SHADOW** made its high-definition debut in Germany under its German title **DIE NACHT DER VAMPIRE**; which contained Spanish and German language options as well as removable German and English subtitles. This "Limited Edition" Blu-ray is currently available on Amazon Germany, but is quite the hefty investment at 33€.

WIZARDS OF THE LOST KINGDOM (p.23) – US video blurb: *"A Boy-Magician On A Fabulous Adventure Through A World Beyond Fantasy."* Released domestically on Beta/VHS in 1986 by Media Home Entertainment, in the UK in the same decade it was put out on PAL VHS/Betamax cassette by Medusa/Channel 5 Video (with the cover tag-line *"On The Far Edge Of Fantasy The Ultimate Conflict Is Drawing Near"*). In the same period, under the title **DEN MAGISKA ZONEN** it was issued in the same tape formats in Sweden by Concorde/Juno Media (JM), in its original English dialogue with Swedish subtitles. On a related note, footage from the film was reused in the kiddie-oriented fantasy **ANDY COLBY'S INCREDIBLE ADVENTURE** (a.k.a. **ANDY AND THE AIRWAVE RANGERS**, 1988, USA, D: Deborah Brock). That patch-job also incorporated sundry excerpts edited in from such other Rog Corman productions as **DEATH RACE 2000** (1975), **EAT MY DUST** (1976), **DEATHSPORT** (1978), **BATTLE BEYOND THE STARS** (1980), **SPACE RAIDERS** (1983) and **CHOPPING MALL** (a.k.a. **KILLBOTS**, 1986, all USA). Both **WOTLK** and its '89 insta-sequel **WIZARDS OF THE LOST KINGDOM II**—the latter in a heavily-shortened version—are available for viewing on YouTube as uploads ripped from their original VHS videocassette versions. Unless you can track down copies of the original tapes themselves, YT is about your only other option for viewing these cheezed-out 1980s fantasy flicks.

THE WOLF MAN (p.63) – Issued on US DVD by Universal during the format's infancy in 1999, it has since been released in numerous collections (all from Universal), including "The Wolf Man: The Legacy Collection", the "Monster Legacy DVD Gift Set" (which also included miniature busts of Dracula, Frankenstein and The Wolf Man), the 4-pack "Classic Monsters: Universal 100th Anniversary Spotlight Collection" and, most recently, as a massive "Universal Classic Monsters Complete 30-film Collection". It has also made the transition to Blu-ray as part of "Universal Classic Monsters: The Essential Collection"; and, for you hardcore collectors, this very same collection was released in the UK in an impressive coffin-shaped box. Finally, for you VHS devotees, Universal released this numerous times in that far-from-dead tape format; the first time in 1987, and even as late as 2001.

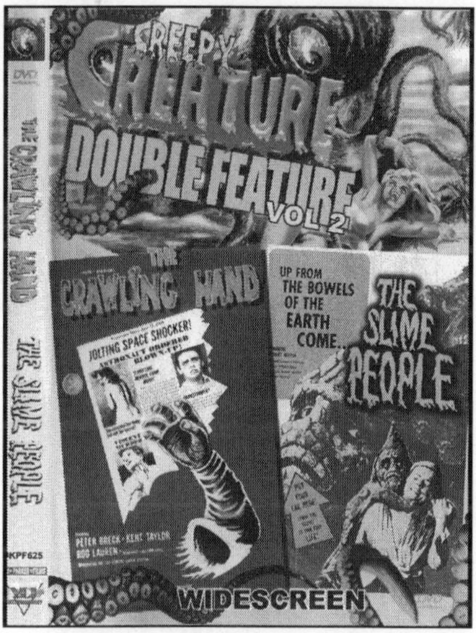

THE SLIME PEOPLE US DVD jacket

13134419R00064

Printed in Great Britain
by Amazon.co.uk, Ltd.,
Marston Gate.